After Tomorrow

Gillian Cross

OXFORD
UNIVERSITY PRESS

A note from the author

All my life I've seen pictures of refugees and I've wondered how it would feel to be driven away from home by a conflict or a natural disaster. Suppose it happened to me? Would I survive?

Normally, I explore difficult questions like that by writing stories. But how could I write about being a refugee? Stories need action and excitement. Whenever I tried to imagine living in a refugee camp, I pictured myself sitting around, waiting for help to arrive. There was no action there.

My problem was that I didn't know anything about how refugees actually live. Then one day a charity asked me to help with putting together an information pack about a refugee camp in Chad. I looked at lots of photographs and read the stories of individual people who'd been forced to leave their homes and find shelter in the camp. And I began to understand what their lives were really like. They did everything they could to help themselves: setting up small businesses, learning new skills and running schools for their children.

Suppose it happened to me, I thought, *or someone I know. Would we manage as well as that?*

The moment I asked myself that question, the character of Matt came jumping into my head. I knew his name, I knew he was a sensible, practical boy – and I knew he was good at mending bikes. Suppose he was forced to leave home? Suppose he had to escape to France, through the Channel Tunnel? What would happen after that? And how would he cope?

I had to find out his story. And that's why I wrote *After Tomorrow*.

I'm very pleased that it's being published in this special edition for Project X *Origins*. It's a book that means a lot to me and I'm delighted that it will have a chance to reach more readers.

Gillian Cross

i

THE FIRST RAID happened on an ordinary, boring evening. We were all sitting round the kitchen table and Mum was serving our tea. It was watery vegetable stew—as usual—and Taco was moaning about the swede.

As usual.

He scowled at the orange lumps on his plate and started singing under his breath. '*Horrible sick for tea today, sick for tea, sick for tea . . .* '

'Now, don't be silly,' Justin said. 'Grandpa grew that swede, Taco. And Mum's cooked it specially for us.'

'It's *sick*,' Taco muttered. He put his head down stubbornly, like a little bull.

'It's food,' Mum said shortly. She ladled some stew on to her own plate and sat down to eat. 'If you don't want yours, give it to Matt. And go to bed.'

I'd have eaten Taco's share like a shot. But I knew he'd spend the whole night moaning about being hungry if I did, so I whispered in his ear. 'Race you! If I finish first, I get to stomp on your shoebox.'

'NO!' roared Taco. (The shoebox trick always worked. No one knew what he kept in there, but it was his treasure.) He grabbed a spoon and started shovelling stew into his mouth.

So it was a normal, dull evening. And then suddenly, without any warning—

CRASH!!!

The back door burst open, splintering away from its hinges, and two men in balaclavas leapt into the kitchen. They were yelling at the tops of their voices.

'OK! Nobody move! Hands on the table!'

'Shut your mouths!'

They were both holding big, heavy wrenches, swinging them round like weapons. Justin began to stand up—and then sank slowly back into his chair. He looked stupid, but it made sense.

If a wrench like that hit you, it wouldn't just give you a bruise.

The men didn't hesitate. One of them grabbed Taco and yanked him backwards in his chair. The other one ripped open the cupboard doors, one after another—until he found the food cupboard.

He started emptying it straight away, scooping out pasta and beans and cereal—all the food Mum had stashed away so carefully. He loaded it all into trolley bags, cramming them full.

'Don't take *everything*,' Justin bleated, when he opened the freezer. 'We've got children to feed.'

'It's your kids or ours, mate,' said the other man.

He swung his wrench high in the air and looked sideways at Justin. Taco's spoon shook, spilling swede back on to the plate, and his eyes opened wide and white.

Justin opened his mouth to argue—and then shut it again, without saying anything.

'That's better,' the man said grimly. 'We don't want any trouble.'

All our frozen food went into the next couple of bags. Beans. Beetroot. Carrots. Apple. Our precious sausages and bacon and the bony bits of lamb for stewing. For a second there was no sound except the thump of frozen meat dropping into the bag. Then Mum put an arm round Taco's shoulders and started whispering in his ear.

The wrench turned towards her. She glanced up at it and stopped talking, but she didn't move her arm.

In fifteen minutes, all the cupboards were bare. The fridge and the freezer were standing empty, with their doors wide open and the ice slowly starting to melt. The man with the bags took them out into the hall and lined them up by the front door. Then he went out—leaving the other one to guard us.

That was our chance! We should have jumped him then. Justin could have knocked him sideways **CRUNCH! THUMP!** and I could have sat on his head while Mum grabbed the wrench. Then we'd have attacked the other man when he came back and **BANG! ZAP!! POW!!!** we would have been in charge. We'd have made them put all our food back and then tied them up and called the police.

My dad would have done that. He would have picked up those weedy little raiders and sorted them out. But Justin didn't move. Not an inch. He went on sitting meekly at the table, watching the wrench.

The other raider started a van outside and reversed it up to the front door—driving straight across the lettuce patch. He jumped out, without bothering to turn off the engine, and loaded the bags into the back of the van. Then he slammed the rear doors and stuck his head back into the kitchen to nod to his mate.

The man with the wrench edged slowly towards the door, watching us all. Ready to race forward if one of us looked like moving. At the last moment, he reached out and swept his hand across all the light switches, plunging us into darkness. Then he raced for the van, slamming the front door behind him.

For a moment we sat without moving, listening to the van drive out on to the road. Then Taco started to make a horrible gasping noise, as if he was suffocating. '*Uh—uh—uh—*'

'It's all right,' Justin said. He snatched Taco out of his chair and hugged him, hard. 'They've gone, Taco. It's all *right*.'

Mum leapt up and charged out of the house, yelling after the van. I think she was trying to see the number plate, but she was way too late for that. All she could do was shout rude words as it hurtled round the corner and disappeared. As the noise of the engine faded, her voice died away too and we heard her turn back towards the house.

Then there was a different kind of shout. More like a scream.

Justin put Taco down and raced for the door. I followed him, with Taco behind me, clutching at my sweatshirt. Mum was standing in the middle of the path, staring back at the house, and her mouth was twisted into a tight little knot. When she saw us, she pointed at the space over the front door.

We ran down the path, turned round to look—and saw huge black letters spray-painted right across the wall.

SCADGERS!

'What's that?' Taco said, in a small, scared voice.

Mum shook her head and pressed her lips together.

'It means *hoarders*.' Justin shuddered. 'Rich, greedy people who buy up all the food and hide it away so they don't have to share it with anyone else.'

'*We're* not rich,' I said. 'And we're not greedy either.'

'They don't care about that,' Mum said. Suddenly she sounded very tired. '*They* think we're scadgers—and they've tagged our house. Labelled us as fair game for any stinking raider who sees that. So this won't be the last time.'

Justin stroked her arm. 'Don't worry, Ali. I've got some paint in the garage. I'll paint over it in the morning. You'd better get on to the insurance people then. And you could phone the police now.'

'What can *they* do?' Mum said bitterly.

But she went inside straight away and rang them. And that made her even crosser. Justin and I were upstairs, putting Taco to bed, and we could hear her shouting.

'What do you *mean* you can't come out? . . . I don't care if it *does* happen fifty times a week . . . It's not our fault you're short-staffed . . . '

Taco sat up in bed, listening to it all. 'Why won't the police come?' he whispered. 'Why is Mum so angry?'

Justin sighed and tried to make him lie down. 'Lots of people are having their food stolen. And there aren't enough police to visit them all.'

'So why don't we get more police?' Taco said.

I knew the answer to that one. 'Because there's not enough money to pay them. The government can't afford it.'

'Why can't they go to the bank and get more money?' Taco said. 'And why did those men come and take our food? Why didn't they get their own? Why—'

Justin looked at me and rolled his eyes. How could we possibly explain all that? We'd need to go back to the beginning, before Taco was even born. Before my dad died and Mum met Justin.

Right back to the day when five banks crashed at once. The Monday they called Armageddon.

2

I'VE NEVER REALLY understood exactly what happened on that Monday, but I know it changed everything.

I didn't know at the time, of course. It was two days before my fourth birthday and the only bank I knew about was my little black and white money box. But, as Mum says, even the grown-ups didn't guess how bad things were going to get.

'Lots of things had crashed before that,' she said, 'and everyone still managed OK. We thought we could carry on the same as before.'

So next morning—the day before my birthday— Dad tweaked my nose, ruffled my hair and said, 'See you tomorrow, Matty. Save me some birthday cake.' Then he went off to Manchester with a truckload of potatoes. The way he did every Tuesday.

Only this time he didn't come back.

His truck was hijacked by a gang. When Dad tried to fight them off, they killed him. A man found him the next day, while he was walking his dog, and the police came round to break the news to Mum.

They knocked on the door just as she was lighting my candles.

I remember those candles. I sat at the table and watched them burn right down to nothing. They made puddles of blue wax on the icing.

Afterwards, Grandpa came to fetch me away. He put me on the back of his bike and wheeled me down the road, across the allotments and in through his back gate—the way he always did.

Grandma Grace must have been OK then, because she gave me a hug and a piece of cake. And Grandpa took me into his shed and let me hang all the tools on their hooks, even the dangerous ones, like the saw and the axe. There were black shapes painted on the wall, to show you where each tool went, and Grandpa gave me a toffee for getting them all right.

My dad was a big man, with a snake tattooed up one arm, across his back and down the other arm. When he hugged me, he pretended to be a boa constrictor, squeezing me to death.

That was only a joke, of course.

Dad loved barbecues. Ribs and steaks. Fish wrapped in foil. Kebabs loaded with big, juicy lumps of meat. Mum made huge bowls of salad and afterwards we had chocolate cake with ice cream and strawberries.

When Dad took us shopping, the supermarket shelves were crammed with packets and tins and there were huge piles of fruit and vegetables. All the freezers were full and once there was a woman handing out samples of cheese for people to taste. *Free.*

Sometimes I dream we're back there, going up and down the aisles. Heaping the trolley with meat and crisps and bananas and sugary doughnuts. But in my dream we never reach the checkout. Before we can finish shopping, all the lights go out. There's a big crash and—

RAA-AA-AA-AAAAR!

A giant black monster, covered in slime, smashes its way in through the supermarket roof. Before we can move, it slithers along the aisles, swallowing everything on the shelves. And when I shout for Dad, he's not there any more.

It's Justin who's pushing the trolley. And all he can do is stare at the monster, with his stupid mouth wide open.

Mum says that's not fair. 'Armageddon Monday changed everything,' she says. 'That's why the hijackers wanted Dad's lorry. They knew food would start running out. Don't you remember what a hard time we had before I married Justin?'

No, I don't remember any of that. I don't remember anything about food being short—until the day Mum came home from the shops and *cried*.

She and Justin were married by then, but Taco was still in a high chair, so I must have been around six. Justin was giving us our tea (slimy pasta with a little bit of grated cheese) and when Mum came through the back door, Taco bounced up and down in his high chair and waved his arms around, shouting, 'Muh! Muh! Muh!'

Mum heaved her shopping bag on to the table, sat down in a chair—and burst into tears.

That was the first time I ever saw her cry. It was *so* not like her, that Justin went flying across the kitchen.

'What's the matter, Ali? What's happened?'

He crouched down and hugged her, but Mum shook her head and sat up straight, pushing him away.

'It was *horrible*,' she said fiercely, still sobbing and catching her breath. 'People were fighting over little pieces of cheese. And do you know what they're asking for chickens now? *Ninety pounds each*. Where's it all going to end?'

Justin looked at the shopping bag on the table. 'Did you manage to get *anything*?'

Mum shrugged. 'A bit more pasta and some apples. And a little loaf of bread. That's not going to last very long, is it?'

Justin peered into the bag, frowning in a useless, silly way. I think he wanted to say something good, so Mum would cheer up, but before he could think of anything Taco started banging his tray and shouting.

'Yes! Grampa! Yes! YES!'

And there was Grandpa outside the back door.

He propped his bicycle against the wall and opened the door. 'Anyone fancy some courgettes?' he said. 'And half a dozen eggs and some carrots?'

Mum laughed, a bit wildly, and stood up. 'Haven't seen you since Wednesday. Thought you'd forgotten us.'

'As if,' Grandpa said. He unstrapped the box from the back of his bike and carried it over to the kitchen table. 'There you are. There'll be pounds of blackcurrants too, in a couple of days. You can have all those if you like. Your mother's not really up to making jam any more.'

'But I *like* Grandma Grace's jam,' I said.

Mum frowned and shook her head at me. 'Can't make jam if there isn't any sugar,' she said to Grandpa.

'A pity you can't swap a few pounds of blackcurrants for a packet of sugar,' Justin said lightly.

He was only joking, of course, but Mum suddenly lit up like a light bulb. 'Hey,' she said. '*Hey!* That's a great idea. You're a genius, Justin!'

'I am?' Justin looked blank. 'What did I say?'

'You said we should swap the fruit we don't need. That's brilliant. There's always more than we can eat—isn't there, Dad? Fruit *and* vegetables.' She looked at Grandpa.

He nodded, cautiously. 'It could be good. But how are you going to find people who've got something to swap?'

Mum grinned. 'I know how to do that! I'll set it up tomorrow.'

The next day was Saturday. As soon as we'd finished breakfast (courgettes on toast) Mum took a load of Grandpa's fruit out of our freezer and went off to see Bob. He owned the haulage firm where Dad used to work and his trucks went all over the place.

When Mum came back, she was smiling.

'Well?' Justin said. 'Did the swapping work? What did you get?'

17

'Nothing!' Mum said. 'I gave all that to Bob.' And she grinned even more.

'You gave away food?' Justin said. '*For nothing?*'

Mum nodded again. 'Had to get Bob on our side, didn't I? And it's worked. The real swapping starts next week.'

She spent the whole of Sunday at Grandpa's, picking courgettes and blackcurrants. There were lettuces too, from his allotment, and new potatoes. When she came back, the car was loaded with boxes and carrier bags.

On Monday morning, she drove down to the yard again. This time, she went very early, while Taco and I were still in bed, and she handed out fruit and vegetables to all the drivers, before they set off for the day.

'See what you can get for these,' she said. 'And keep some for yourselves.'

It worked like magic. Fresh fruit and vegetables had almost disappeared from the shops, but lots of people had things in their store cupboards—and they were delighted to swap. It was never very much at a time, but the drivers brought back something every week and gradually it mounted up.

Packets of flour and rice. Tins of beans and pieces of cheese and cartons of long life milk. We hadn't seen things like that for months.

But Mum wouldn't let us eat them all. 'We have to *store* these,' she said. 'In case things get worse.'

So gradually—one packet and tin at a time—our food cupboard started filling up. And then one of the drivers found a farmer who was ready to swap meat for flour and sugar. So some of the packets came out of the cupboard and we had joints of meat in the freezer.

Mum and Justin started growing vegetables in our garden as well, so there was more to swap. For the next few years, we always had plenty to eat—even if it was mostly vegetable stew. There was food on our plates every day and enough stashed away in the kitchen to last six months or more.

I heard some of the kids at school talking about being hungry and I knew I was really lucky. It was a good, safe feeling. We could look after ourselves.

And that was what Mum said after the raid. 'The police won't come and the insurance won't pay out. So—we have to look after ourselves. No one else is going to do it.'

She made Justin fit new locks on the doors and they made a secret store cupboard under the stairs, hidden behind a false wall. Mum was determined the raiders weren't going to catch us out again. She knew things were getting worse all the time.

It was on the News every evening.

Two or three times a week, there were interviews with families who'd been raided. But they were much worse off than us. You could see that, by their desperate, frightened faces. *What are we going to do?* they said. *There's no food in the shops. How are we going to survive?*

On the days when there was nothing about raids on the News, there were usually pictures of riots. The riots started in London, but soon they were happening all over the country. Crowds of angry people marched through the cities with banners saying **STOP THE SCADGERS** and **OUTLAW HOARDING!** They broke into shops and warehouses and grabbed whatever they could find.

Taco insisted on watching it all.

Mum tried to stop him, of course. But every time she turned the TV off, he screamed and screamed until she put it on again. He was obsessed with the News. And every time he saw pictures of people in masks, he thought it was the men who'd raided our house.

'Are they coming here?' he'd say. 'Where's Luton?' (Or Birmingham, or Edinburgh, or wherever the latest report was about.) 'Are they coming back?'

Justin always said no. 'They're hundreds of miles away, Taco. And I've painted over that nasty graffiti. We're absolutely safe now. They won't come here again.'

That was rubbish, of course. Yes, there was white paint on top of those ugly black letters, but they were already showing through again. I could see them, and so could Taco. No wonder he was afraid. When I went up to bed, he was never asleep now, like he used to be. He was always wide awake, staring into the dark. Listening for the next raid. And I listened too, planning what I would do next time the raiders came.

But things never happen the way you expect.

3

THE NEXT GANG of raiders didn't come at night. And they didn't come to our house. They turned up at the allotments, one sunny afternoon when Taco and I were at school.

There was no one at the allotments except Grandpa and his friend Les Bennett. Grandpa was over the far side, hoeing round his beans, but Les had finished work. He hung around for a few minutes, chatting to Grandpa, and then walked off towards the gate.

He was nearly there when a couple of cars came screeching in, almost knocking him over. They pulled up and half a dozen men jumped out. Les yelled to Grandpa, telling him to get away.

But Grandpa wouldn't abandon his precious vegetables. That's how he was. He didn't give in to anyone.

When he saw the raiders, he waved his hoe in the air, shouting at them to keep away from his patch.

Les said they just laughed at him.

By the time the police arrived, the raiders had gone. They'd trampled all over the allotments and taken everything worth eating. Grandpa was lying face down on top of his beans.

The doctor told us he'd died of a heart attack.

After that, everything changed again. Once Grandpa was dead, Mum and Justin realized how much he'd done to look after Grandma Grace. Because she needed it.

'She can't live on her own,' Mum said. 'Not the way she is now. And I'm not putting her into a home— even if we could find one that's still open. She's my mother and I'll look after her myself.'

Our house was too small for Grandma Grace to come and live with us, so we all moved in with her instead. (And I *still* had to share a room with Taco.) Mum decided that growing vegetables was more useful than going out to work, so she gave up her job and took over Grandpa's garden and the allotment.

She and Justin dug up the garden. They got rid of the roses, broke up the patio and chopped the decking into firewood. They planted vegetables everywhere and Mum started looking out for some more chickens.

'I can't manage it all on my own,' she said. 'Everyone has to help.'

That meant Taco and Justin and me. After that, if I wanted to play football on Saturdays I had to get up at six o'clock—so I could do three hours weeding before I left. Taco had to pick the sprouts and empty the compost bucket and Justin spent most evenings on the allotment, after work.

How had Grandpa managed it all on his own, without any help?

Sometimes I went into his shed and stared at the rows of tools behind the workbench. They were still hanging neatly in their places on the wall—all except the tools he used for maintaining his bike. Those were in a big canvas roll, with loops and pockets to keep everything tidy—spare brake pads and inner tubes, tyre levers and Allen keys, gear cables and spanners and handlebar tape. Everything he needed was there, all neatly organized.

I knew those tools too. They reminded me of all the time I'd spent watching Grandpa work on the bike. He always made sure I could see what he was doing and he liked it when I asked questions. I thought about that a lot and sometimes I took the tools out of their roll and laid them along the bench, making myself remember what each one was and how to use it.

One day, Mum came in while I was standing there. I thought she was going to shout at me, because I should have been picking beans. But she didn't. She stood and looked at the workbench for a moment, without saying anything.

Then she grinned. 'You're nearly as tall as he was now. I reckon you could ride his bike, if you adjust the saddle.'

The bike was on its stand in a corner of the shed. Getting dusty. I looked across at it.

'Think so?' I said.

Mum nodded. 'Let's get it out tomorrow. If you fix it up, you could hitch on that little trailer of his and take the vegetables down to Bob's. Save me a bit of petrol.' She patted my arm and went off to dig up some carrots.

I didn't just raise the saddle. I stripped down the whole bike. All it really needed was one new brake pad and a bit of polish, but I wanted to make sure I remembered everything. So I oiled the chain and lubricated the gear cables. Then I replaced both brake pads, realigned the front wheel and cleaned the whole thing until it glittered.

The shed was full of cobwebs and dust, so I covered the bike with old sacks when I wasn't using it. It looked as though there was nothing there except a heap of rubbish and I loved pulling off the sacks and seeing the gleam of the bike in its dark corner.

I kept the tool roll under my bed. Don't ask me why. It was like Taco, I suppose, with his precious shoebox. If something's really important, it's good to have it stashed away in a safe place. I wished I could take the bike up there too.

I'd been delivering vegetables to Bob for a couple of months when the real disaster happened.

It started with a massive crash in the middle of the night. I woke up with a jump and heard lots of shouting and thudding downstairs. Taco was already halfway across the room, even though he wasn't properly awake. I grabbed him and pulled him into bed with me, tucking the duvet round to stop him shivering.

'Is it the raiders?' he whimpered. 'Have they come back?'

There was another crash and a sound of breaking glass. (Was that the TV or the computer screen?)

'Don't worry,' I whispered. 'They'll just take the food and go away. Like last time.' I crossed my fingers in the dark, hoping it was true.

Taco snuggled closer, with his elbows in my chest. 'They won't come up here?'

'Not if we stay quiet,' I said. I listened to the noises, trying to work out what was going on.

'I'm *scared*,' Taco said. His voice was starting to wobble. 'I don't want to stay here. I want Mum.'

I tried to keep him quiet, but that just got him more upset. So I gave in and slipped out of bed. 'All right. Let's go and find her.'

Taco grabbed at my arm. 'But suppose they hear us? Suppose—?'

'No supposing,' I said. 'Come *on*.'

'Wait a minute,' Taco muttered. He shot across the room and grovelled under his bed for the shoebox. He hugged it to his chest and we darted across the landing to Mum's room.

She and Justin were out of bed too. Justin was half-dressed, and Mum was hanging on to his shoulders to stop him going downstairs.

'Don't be stupid,' she was saying. 'How will we manage if you get yourself hurt?'

'Someone should stop them,' Justin said. (But he didn't shake her off, the way Dad would have done.)

Taco ran across the room and flung himself at Mum's knees. 'They won't come up here, will they? They won't come and get us?'

Mum sat down on the bed and pulled him on to her lap. 'It's all right,' she whispered. 'It's OK.' She cuddled him and buried her face in his hair.

But it wasn't OK. A couple of minutes later, we heard heavy feet thumping up the stairs. Mum put an arm round me too.

'Keep quiet!' she whispered. 'Don't annoy them.'

The raiders headed straight for us, flinging the door open so hard it crashed into the wall. There were half a dozen of them. Heavy, tall men with packs on their backs.

There was a second of silence, as if the world stopped moving. Then Mum said, 'You won't find any food in here.'

The men didn't bother to reply. They rampaged through the room, wrenching the cupboards open and pulling out all the drawers.

They'd just started on the wardrobe when Grandma Grace suddenly appeared in the doorway. 'What's going on?' she said plaintively. 'Are they making a film, Alison?'

A raider whirled round and made a horrible snarling noise.

'For goodness' *sake*!' Mum said angrily. 'Can't you see she's got dementia? She doesn't know what she's saying.' She went across the room and hugged Grandma Grace, as if the raider wasn't there.

'You want to keep your wife in order,' the man growled at Justin. 'Or she'll get you all in trouble.'

The others were going through Mum's jewellery box, but there was nothing there worth stealing. One of them gave a quick, impatient nod—*Let's get out*—and they headed for the door. But just when we thought it was over, the last one turned round in the doorway.

He whipped out his phone—and *photographed* us all.

'What's that for?' Mum said sharply.

Justin pulled at her arm. 'Alison—be careful.'

'I want to know what he's *doing*,' Mum said. 'He can't just—'

The man laughed nastily, waving his phone in her face. 'Going to be internet stars, aren't you, darling? Take a look at yourselves on ScadgePost—when your computer's fixed.'

The others roared with laughter and Mum started forward, reaching for the phone. 'What do you mean? Give me that!'

'No!' Justin said. 'Alison—'

He caught hold of Mum's arm, to pull her back, but it was too late. Suddenly the men weren't laughing any more. And they weren't leaving either. They were pushing their way back into the room and grabbing at Mum and Justin.

Grandma Grace started screaming and the men laughed again, but it was a different kind of laughter now, fierce and ugly, and Justin was shouting and throwing himself at them, and I didn't know what was happening and—

And then Mum said, very loud and clear, 'Matthew! Taco! Don't look. *Shut your eyes, both of you!*'

I pulled Taco's head into my lap and leaned across him, dragging the duvet over us both and tugging it round tightly. And then—

I did what Mum said.

I didn't look. I didn't see anything.

Nothing at all.

After a long time, Mum came and lifted the duvet away. 'It's all right,' she said. 'They've gone.'

Justin was over on the other side of the room, leaning against the doorframe. He turned round and there was blood running down his face from a big, jagged cut underneath his right eye. Something had happened to his cheek as well, because it was a weird shape. And he was crying.

Mum heaved a long, slow sigh. Then she went across the room and put her arms round him, heaving them into place as if they were almost too heavy to lift.

'We're still alive,' she said. 'That's the main thing.'

Justin dropped his head on to her shoulder, leaving a bloodstain on her dressing gown. 'I'm useless,' he said.

'Don't talk about it,' Mum said wearily. She looked round for Grandma Grace and gave her a bright, brittle smile. 'Everything's fine, Mother. You can go back to bed now.'

Grandma Grace gave her a long, puzzled stare. Then she shuffled off to her bedroom and Mum turned to Taco and me.

'No!' I said quickly. 'I don't want to go back to bed. Please, Mum. I need to see what they've done downstairs.'

She hesitated for a moment and then nodded, as if it was too much effort to argue. 'All right. Let's go and look at the damage.'

4

THEY'D TRASHED EVERYTHING. The floor was a mess of broken crockery and glass and half the windows were smashed. So were the computer screen and the big TV. They'd missed the little TV in the kitchen, but the cupboard doors were all wrenched off their hinges and the fridge was lying on its side in a pool of water.

Empty, of course.

They were all empty.

But it wasn't only food they'd taken. The DVD player had gone too. And my mobile phone (*stupid* to leave it downstairs) and the Sky box and the DS and all the remote controls. They'd stripped the house of everything that was new enough to trade, and destroyed all the rest.

'*Why?*' Justin said. There was still blood running down his cheek and his face was starting to swell up. 'What's the point of breaking things?'

Mum shook her head wearily. 'They're angry,' she said. 'Angry and afraid—and they hate us.' She picked up a cloth and rinsed it under the tap. 'Come here and let me look at that cut.'

Justin turned towards her, but when she dabbed at the cut he caught his breath and pushed her away. 'Leave it for now,' he said. 'It's nothing.' He'd gone very pale, as if he was going to faint.

Mum peered at the cut. 'There might be something broken. We should go to hospital.'

'No—it's nothing.' Justin shook his head—and winced again. 'I'll go to hospital in the morning. We've got to clear up this mess now.'

It was freezing cold, because of all the broken windows. Justin found some boards in the garage and nailed them over the worst holes. Then he turned on the heating to warm the house up. But nothing happened. He spent half an hour fiddling with the boiler—and then he realized why.

The raiders hadn't just smashed their way round our house. They'd been in the garden too. And they'd cut through the outflow pipe of our oil tank and drained off all the oil. The tank was empty.

Mum made Taco a hot water bottle and he went back to bed. But I put on my coat and helped with the clearing up. As I swept up the broken glass in the kitchen, I kept wondering if the raiders had broken into the shed as well.

What had they taken from there?

As soon as it was light, I went down the garden. When I saw the shed door hanging open, I knew the raiders had been there. The lawnmower was gone and so was the big wheelbarrow.

And all the tools from the wall.

I stood for a moment, staring at the black painted shapes where they should have been. Remembering how careful Grandpa was about hanging them up when he'd finished using them. I think I was putting off the moment when I had to look in the corner at the back of the shed, but I forced myself to go and move the sacks.

And the bike was still there! They hadn't found it.

I could hardly believe it. I ran my hands over the frame, to see if they'd damaged it somehow, but it was all fine, even the tyres. They simply hadn't bothered to see what was under the sacks.

By then, Mum was shouting for me to come in and get ready for school—as if it was an ordinary day. I pushed the bike back into its corner and dumped some old cardboard boxes on top of it, under the sacks, to make it look even more like rubbish. Then I went back into the kitchen.

Mum was in hyperdrive. That's how she deals with trouble. As soon as I walked in, she pushed me towards the stairs. 'Go and clean yourself up. You can't go to school like that. And make sure Taco's out of bed. Move!'

Taco was sitting on the bedroom floor, cradling his shoebox on his lap. 'I'm not leaving this at home,' he said. 'They might come back while we're at school. I'm taking it with me.'

'Please yourself,' I said. No good trying to boss him around. 'It'll be safer here, though. The raiders didn't care about it, did they? But the kids at school will want to see inside. They'll make you take the lid off.'

His mouth opened into a silent O. He crawled across the room and slid the box back under his bed. Then he grabbed his towel and raced into the bathroom, before I could get ahead of him.

As soon as he'd gone, I knelt down and scrabbled under my own bed for the tool roll. It didn't need checking—I knew everything was still there—but I wanted to *see* the tools. Feel the coldness of the metal and the smooth, powdery surfaces of the spare inner tubes.

At least they made sense, even if everything else was going wrong.

When I came downstairs again, Mum and Justin were arguing. She wanted to drive him to the hospital, and he wouldn't let her.

'You've got enough to cope with,' he said. 'Grace is bound to be in a state when she wakes up. I'll drive myself. And maybe the boys should stay at home today, so they can help you.'

'*No!*' Mum said fiercely. 'They're not going to miss school. As long as it manages to stay open, they're going to be there.'

She almost pushed us out of the house. Then, when we reached the pavement, she came running after us.

'Keep your mouths shut about what happened last night,' she said in a low voice. 'I don't want people knowing. They might think we deserved it.'

A month or two ago, not telling would have been really hard. My best friends always knew if I wasn't OK. They'd have got the whole story out of me by the end of morning break.

But they weren't at school any more. They'd disappeared, like lots of other kids—and some of the teachers too. When the raids started getting serious, Tiny's parents had whisked him off to his grandparents' flat in Spain. And Luke's dad had found a job on a farm, somewhere in France, and taken the whole family out there.

I'd had texts from them both of course, but they hadn't bothered to tell me their addresses. So now my phone was gone I couldn't get in touch with them. Not till they came back to England.

At least that made it easy to keep quiet at school.

I spent the whole day going over and over the raid in my mind. The word that I kept coming back to was—*ScadgePost*. What was it? What did it mean?

I tried to get on a computer at school, so I could find out, but there were only four computers left by then. (I think the teachers had traded the rest.) Anyway the internet connection was down. Of course. So when I picked Taco up, at the end of the day, I made him run all the way to the library, so we could get on the internet there.

We just made it in time. The computers were all booked from four o'clock, but the librarian said I could have ten minutes. Maximum. I made Taco stand behind me—so no one else could see the screen—and then I searched as fast as I could.

About a million results came up, mostly from people saying *ScadgePost* was brilliant. I didn't waste any time on those. Just went straight to the home page—and up came a map of the whole country, with a banner across the top.

ScadgeSpot—see where your local scadgers are hiding!

Taco leaned over my shoulder. 'What is it?' he said. 'What are you doing?'

'Sssh!' I said. 'Tell you in a moment.' I zoomed in on the map, found our town and clicked.

That was all it took. One click. Immediately the screen filled with dozens of photos, all with details attached. Names. Dates. Addresses. Everything.

And we were there already, right at the top.

All five of us were in the picture, and we looked like criminals. Mum's face was blurred, because she'd moved her head, and Grandma Grace was staring down at the floor, but Justin, Taco, and I were completely recognizable—under a caption that said, *Guilty!*

Taco caught his breath and clutched at my shoulder and I shut the window down as fast as I could. When I looked up at him, he was shivering.

'Don't worry,' I said. Trying to sound calm. 'Maybe no one really looks at *ScadgePost*. Maybe no one's heard of it.'

But I knew that wasn't true.

When we told Mum, she went straight down to the library herself, without even putting her coat on. When she came back, she was furious—and she started shouting at Justin.

'I *knew* we ought to get out! I told you *three months ago*, didn't I? And you said *Wait and see* and *Things might get better*. But I was right! If we'd left then, we'd be safe in France now—not waiting for the next lot of thugs to pick us off that horrible website.'

Taco was staring at the little kitchen TV, waiting for the News. He looked round and blinked at Mum. '*France?* How can we go there?'

'You'll go wherever I tell you!' Mum snapped. She started banging round the kitchen, peeling some old carrots she'd found in the garden.

'Things aren't so great in France,' Justin said. 'They've got problems too, you know.'

Mum put the carrots down and chopped them into slices, crashing the knife down hard. 'They may not have much food, but at least they've got law and order.'

Taco was frowning. 'We can't go to France. We—'

I nudged him, to make him shut up. 'It'll be like Joe,' I said. That was Taco's best friend. 'He's gone to France, hasn't he?'

'But we can't speak French,' Taco muttered.

Grandma Grace was sitting at the kitchen table opposite us. She'd been staring at the pattern on the cloth, but suddenly she lifted her head. '*Parlez-vous,*' she said brightly. Then she drummed her fingers on the arm of her chair and started singing in a thin, high voice.

'*Alouette, gentille alouette,*
Alouette, je te plumerai . . . '

Mum ignored us all and went on talking to Justin. 'I'm going down to the yard, first thing in the morning. Bob's still got trucks going over to France. He'll know what to do.'

'Let's not rush into anything,' Justin said feebly. He looked terrible. His face was purple and swollen now, pulled into crinkles by the stitches they'd put in at the hospital. They'd sewn him up in a hurry and told him his cheekbone would have to heal up by itself. 'We need to look at all the options.'

'*Auprès de ma blonde,*' Grandma Grace sang softly. '*Qu-il fait bon, fait bon, fait bon . . .* '

Mum scowled at Justin. 'There *aren't* any other options. It's too hard to get in anywhere else. We have to get Bob to take us to France and—'

'*He's* French,' Grandma Grace interrupted triumphantly, pointing at the TV.

'Please!' Mum was really frazzled by now. She put her hands over her ears and raised her voice. 'If you could just be *quiet* while I—'

'Hang on,' Justin said. He leaned past her and turned up the sound on the TV.

On the screen was a large man talking in a foreign language. *We are unable to cope with the flood of applications,* said a translator's voice over the top.

Then the picture changed and we were looking at a long line of people trudging down a country road.

They were loaded down with bundles and backpacks and babies and they all looked miserable and exhausted. *Refugees*, I thought automatically.

But they weren't. They were people like us.

'Where are they?' I said. 'What's happened?'

'Sssh!' Mum waved her hand at me. 'I need to listen.'

The picture changed back to the man we'd seen in the beginning. For a few seconds there was more foreign babble—*malheureusement . . .*—and then the translator's voice came in again.

'The people of France have great sympathy with their British cousins, but these are hard times for our country. We cannot afford to receive the great numbers of people who are trying to enter France. Therefore, with great regret, we must follow the example of other European countries and close our borders . . . '

' . . . *pour éviter une catastrophe encore plus grave en France,*' the French voice finished.

Mum muttered a rude word and glared at the screen.

'What's the matter?' asked Taco.

'We're too late,' Mum said bitterly. 'France isn't going to let in any more of us. So we're stuck here.'

Justin frowned. 'Are you *sure* that's what he meant?'

'Of course I'm sure,' Mum snapped. 'We've ummed and aahed too long and now we've missed our chance. All we can do is stay here and grow vegetables—for other people to steal.' She picked up another carrot

41

and chopped down on it so hard that half of it shot across the floor.

'Alison, don't throw your food around!' Grandma Grace said sharply. She picked up the carrot and started chewing it.

I thought Mum was going to cry then.

Justin put an arm round her shoulders. 'Come on, Ali. It's not like you to give up. Why don't you go and see Bob anyway? Maybe he'll have some ideas.'

'He can't solve all our problems,' Mum said bitterly. But she wiped her eyes with the back of her hand and started peeling the rest of the carrots.

That's all there was for breakfast the next morning as well. Carrots. They were the only things the raiders had left in the garden.

Mum held out a handful to Justin as he came into the kitchen. 'Have some *delicious* breakfast,' she said sarcastically.

Justin took a couple of carrots, but he didn't sit down. 'I'd better go to work,' he said. 'While I've still got a job—just about.'

He looked even worse than the day before, but he went off chewing one of the carrots. Taco and I sat and watched Mum. She was leaning on the draining board and staring down into the sink.

Then Grandma Grace shuffled into the kitchen, holding out her shoes. 'Alison,' she said vaguely, 'I can't work out which foot is which.'

Mum blinked and came back to life. 'Sit down,' she said. 'I'll do it. And then we'll go for a walk.'

Grandma Grace looked round the kitchen and frowned. 'Have I had my breakfast?'

'*Ages* ago,' Mum said lightly. 'Porridge and eggs and bacon. *And* toast. You could do with a bit of exercise after all that food. Let's walk down to school with Matthew and Taco. Then we'll go and have a chat with Bob.'

Grandma Grace beamed. She loved going to the yard. Even when Bob was really busy, he always took a few minutes off to make her laugh.

One visit to Bob. That was all it took. By the time we came home in the afternoon, Mum had everything sorted.

Justin must have left work early, because he was home before us. And the hall was full of luggage. Two suitcases were standing at the bottom of the stairs and Justin was kneeling beside the big rucksack, tying water bottles on to the straps.

'*There* you are,' Mum said as Taco and I walked in. 'You need to get a move on. I want everything packed and ready to go before we have tea.'

Taco looked suspiciously at the rucksack. 'Ready to go where?'

'Tell you at tea time,' Mum said briskly. 'When you've sorted out what you're taking. There's a backpack on each of your beds. I've packed some of your clothes, but there's a bit of room in the top. So if there's *one thing* you really want to take—'

Taco shot upstairs before she could finish. No prizes for guessing what his *one thing* was going to be.

I knew what I wanted too. But it wasn't going to fit in the backpack. 'I'm taking Grandpa's bike,' I said. 'And the tool roll.'

Mum shook her head impatiently. 'Don't be silly. I meant something *small.*'

'I don't care,' I said. 'I'm taking the bike.'

Justin sat back on his heels and looked up at us. 'Actually it's not a bad idea,' he said. 'The bike could be really useful.'

'Bob won't let him take it,' Mum said. 'You know what he's like. He told me we could only have one bag each—and he hates being messed around.'

'He might make an exception.' Justin tied the last knot and pulled the straps tight. 'There's acres of room in those trucks. Let's give it a try. And if he says no, we'll just leave the bike behind.'

Mum hesitated. 'This truck's our last chance, you know. We *have* to be on it. But—well, as long as you don't start arguing with Bob—'

'Thanks!' I said.

I dashed out to the shed to fetch the bike, before she could change her mind. There was no point in taking it into the house, so I hid it behind the front hedge, ready to grab at the last moment. Then I went upstairs to squeeze the tool roll into my bag. I was determined to take that too, even if I had to leave all my clothes behind.

5

SOMEHOW MUM HAD found some more food. I don't know what she'd traded, but when I went downstairs she was in the kitchen spooning out a strange, thick soup. And Justin was cramming a bag of dried pasta into his coat pocket.

Grandma Grace and Taco sat at the table, watching the soup glop on to their plates.

'What *is* it?' Taco said, in a dangerous voice.

'It's *food*.' Mum's voice was even more dangerous. 'And you're going to eat every mouthful, Taco Bannister. It'll be a very long time to your next meal.'

'Will that be France?' Taco said.

Grandma Grace beamed. 'Gay Paree. That's where I had my honeymoon. We went up the Eiffel Tower.'

'I don't think we'll be doing *that*,' Mum said. She sat down and picked up her spoon. 'We *are* going to France, though. But it's a secret. So no sneaky texts to your friends, Matt.' She gave me a sharp look.

'Haven't got a phone, have I?' I started on my soup. I still couldn't tell what was in it, but it tasted OK.

'No texts on *anyone's* phone,' Mum said. 'We're going in one of Bob's trucks, with some other people, and it's *got* to be secret.'

I didn't understand. 'I thought they weren't letting anyone else into France.'

'That's right,' Mum said drily. 'Now you see why it's got to be secret.'

My heart gave a thump. 'So how are we—?'

Mum frowned and shook her head. Meaning, *Don't ask that question*. 'Leave it up to Bob,' she said. 'He's driving the truck himself—and it won't be the only one. There are hundreds of them going tonight. Maybe thousands. This is a last dash, before the Tunnel shuts down, and it's a big operation. They've paid off all the security people at this end so they don't check us.'

'Sounds expensive.' Justin looked at his plate. 'How much did you give Bob?'

Mum shrugged. 'Does it matter? The important thing is—we're going. Bob's picking us up at three o'clock tomorrow morning and we must be ready.'

* * *

After tea, Taco and I had to go to bed. 'Might as well get some sleep,' Mum said. 'But keep your clothes on. If we're not ready and waiting when Bob comes, he'll go without us.'

I slid under my duvet, but I didn't go to sleep. Just lay there for hours, staring through the narrow gap between the curtains. There was a street light outside and a view of Mrs Donovan's house across the road. When would I see that again?

I was still awake when Mum came back and turned on the light. 'Time to get up,' she said. 'I'll go and sort out Grandma Grace. You'll have to deal with Taco. Make sure he goes to the toilet. It's going to be a long journey.'

She shook Taco's shoulder and he sat up, still half-asleep. 'It's important,' he mumbled. 'It's really important—'

'It's important to get *up*,' Mum said. 'No messing about.' She nodded at me in a way that meant *get on with it*—and went off to Grandma Grace's room.

I hauled Taco out of bed and hustled him into the bathroom. I thought we were moving super-fast, but Mum was even faster with Grandma Grace. They were both downstairs before us. Grandma Grace was sitting beside the suitcases, looking dozy and confused, Justin was squashing yet more things into the rucksack and Mum was at the door, watching for the truck. As we came downstairs, she turned round and nodded.

'He's here! Let's go!'

The truck pulled up outside, blocking the light from the street lamp opposite and Justin hoisted the big rucksack on to his back and grabbed the cases.

Grandma Grace looked up at Mum. 'I just need to go to the toilet,' she said cheerfully.

I thought Mum was going to shake her. 'I *asked* you,' she said. 'We can't—'

Justin put a hand on her arm. 'Don't panic. I'll take the boys out and put them on the truck. That should give you time to take her, if you're quick.' He looked round at Taco and me. 'Come on, you two.'

I slipped my backpack on to my shoulder, trying not to think about how heavy it was. 'Here we go, Taco,' I said cheerfully. And the three of us walked down the garden path together.

Bob was waiting for us, with the curtain side of the truck rolled open a little way, to let us in. He peered at Justin. 'Ali said they'd made a mess of your face. Hope you walloped them back.'

Justin gave him a pale smile but before he could reply Bob was looking past him.

'Where's Alison?' he said. 'And her mother.'

'They're on their way,' Justin muttered. 'Be here in a second.'

Bob frowned and tapped his watch. 'I told Ali. *We can't wait around*, I said. If they're not here in one minute—'

'They're coming.' Justin glanced over his shoulder, anxiously, and then grinned. 'Look—here they are!'

Mum was hurrying Grandma Grace through the door, waving at Bob to show they were almost there. I took a step towards the hedge. Time to fetch the bike out. It looked as though we'd be off in a couple of minutes.

And then Grandma Grace tripped over the doorstep.

She fell into the onion patch and as she hit the ground she began to scream. Mum leapt across and knelt down beside her.

'We'll be there in a minute,' she called. 'Hang on.'

She put her arms under Grandma Grace's shoulders, trying to heave her back on to her feet. But every time Grandma Grace moved, even a little bit, there was another terrible scream. Bob made an impatient noise and went hurrying up the path, with Justin right behind him.

Now! I thought. It was the perfect time to sneak the bike on to the truck. Letting go of Taco's hand, I nipped behind the hedge to fetch it. While everyone was distracted, I lifted the bike and rammed it through the gap in the curtain, pushing it into the truck.

'Hey!' yelled an angry voice from inside. But whoever it was caught hold of the bike and pulled it in. I muttered, 'Thank you,' and then turned round to see what was happening in the garden.

Grandma Grace was still screaming. And Bob was standing over her, shaking his head.

'Looks like she's broken something,' I heard him say. 'I'm sorry, Ali, but I can't take her like that. It's not fair on the others.'

'What are we supposed to do?' Justin said. 'We can't leave her behind.'

Bob shrugged. 'That's your problem, mate. You can all stay if you like. But this truck's leaving in three minutes.'

Justin hesitated and Mum stood up and gave him a push. 'Go!' she said. 'We've got to get the boys out of here.'

'But we can't leave Grace.' Justin looked confused. 'She'll never cope on her own.'

'She won't *be* on her own, will she?' Mum snapped. 'Now—get on that truck, before it's too late.'

I didn't know what she meant—but Justin did. 'No!' he said. '*No*, Ali! You've got to come with us!'

Mum shook her head, stubbornly. 'She's my mother and I'm going to look after her. But I'm not going to see the rest of you suffer. *Get my boys on to that truck!*'

Justin caught at her arm. 'I *can't* leave you here. Who'll look after you if the house gets raided again?

Mum didn't even answer him. She shook off his hand and marched down the path behind Bob—leaving Grandma Grace moaning in the onion patch. Justin hovered for a moment and then ran after them.

Mum was determined to see us on to the truck. 'Come on, Taco,' she said briskly. 'Upsadaisy.' She picked him up and almost threw him in. Then she gave me a nudge. 'Go on, Matt. This is your last chance.'

'We can't go without you,' I said.

'Rubbish!' Mum started picking up our bags and lobbing them into the truck, on top of Taco. 'Stop arguing! You're going, and that's it. Here—Justin!'

He came up behind her and the two of them picked me up and pushed me through the curtain. Taco yelped and I landed on top of the suitcases. It was too dark to see much, but I found the bike and squeezed in beside it, right in the corner.

The truck was crammed full, with shadows huddled all round us. It was too dark to be sure which were cases and which were people—until you bumped against them—but I could hear lots of impatient whispering.

Justin peered through the gap. 'What's going on, Bob?' I heard him say angrily. 'You told Ali there would be a *few* other people. But you've filled the whole truck. There's hardly room for us.'

'Can't turn people down, can you?' Bob said. 'You're not the only ones who are desperate. Now— are you coming?'

'*Yes*,' Mum said. 'Yes, they are.' She hugged Justin fiercely and then pushed him at the truck. '*Go!*' she said. 'Before you ruin everything.'

Justin hesitated for a second and then scrambled in, hauling himself over our cases. He was still trying to squeeze in beside Taco when Mum leaned into the truck.

'Here!' she said urgently. She was waving something in her hand and she pushed it at me, because I was nearest. 'Put this somewhere safe.'

It was too dark to see what she'd given me. It felt like a thick bundle of paper with a rubber band around it. I pushed it into the top of my backpack and buckled the flap down over it.

I was just going to say goodbye to Mum when Bob grabbed her shoulders. 'That's enough!' he said. 'We must leave now or we'll never make it. If you're not coming, Ali, get out of the way.' He pulled her backwards on to the pavement.

'Love you all!' she shouted. 'Take care of each other! And phone me when you get to France!'

'Of course we'll phone!' Justin shouted back. 'And—Ali—'

But it was too late to say anything else. Bob was closing the curtain. We heard him buckle it into place and then the engine started up and the truck pulled away from the kerb.

A hand came out of the darkness and tapped my arm. 'Tuck your legs under the ropes, darling,' said a woman's voice. 'And hold on to that bike, or it'll go flying. When Bob gets going, he won't hang about.'

She turned on her torch and shone it at the floor of the truck. There were thick ropes running across it, tied to the lashing rings on either side. We worked our legs underneath the nearest rope and held on tightly as the truck swung out into the road.

'Good luck!' Mum yelled from outside. 'Don't forget to phone!'

My face was jammed right up against the curtain side of the truck. I could see light coming through a little hole just below my chin and I wriggled my head down until my eye was level with it. For a couple of seconds I saw Mum standing under the street lamp. She wasn't waving. She was standing perfectly still, watching the truck disappear down the road.

I stared at her until we swung round the bend and I couldn't see her any more. The truck roared on, past places I saw every day—the corner shop where we bought our comics and sweets, the swing park with the quarter pipe, the flats where Tiny lived till he went to Spain. Then all that was gone and we were out on the motorway.

Trucks aren't meant for passengers. Even with the ropes to cling on to, we kept sliding sideways against each other. At first I kept saying, 'Sorry! Sorry!' But you can't apologize all the time. After half an hour or so I gave up. I just hung on to the bike and the rope and wished I could fall asleep, like Taco.

Two or three times Justin put his mouth against my ear and yelled 'OK?' but it was too noisy to talk properly. The jolting made my bones ache and every time I wriggled, to get a bit more comfortable, people smacked at my legs because my feet were hitting them.

It felt as though the journey was going on for ever. And then—quite suddenly—the truck slowed right down. Stopped. Started. Stopped again.

'What is it?' said a voice out of the darkness. 'Have we reached the tunnel?'

There was a lot of shouting and hooting outside. I could hear big, powerful engines revving all around us and doors slamming as drivers jumped in and out of their cabs. But I couldn't *see* anything. When I peered through my peephole, it was blocked by the side of the truck next to us.

Justin leaned over and whispered into my ear. 'I think we're near the tunnel. Let's hope we make it on to the train. Fingers crossed!'

I'd never been through the tunnel, but I'd looked at pictures of the big freight cars that took the trucks—long cages, with heavy bars along the sides. I'd tried to imagine my dad, driving into one of those—and now I was there myself. I could hear the rumble of the trucks ahead of us driving on to the train.

Stop. Start. Stop.

Everyone round us was super-quiet now—as if they were all holding their breath. The silence woke Taco up and he clutched his bag and burrowed his head into Justin's chest.

Start. Stop. Start—and then the rumbling was underneath us and all around and *we* were the ones driving on to the train. Taco opened his mouth to ask a question, but Justin put a hand over it and shook his head.

Rumble, rumble, rumble. Stop.

And then doors slamming and the sound of footsteps as the drivers left their cabs and headed for the passenger coach.

As Bob walked by the side of our truck, he leaned close to the curtain and whispered—right by my ear. 'We'll be on our way very soon. Stay quiet. Pass it on.'

I whispered the message to Justin and it went from person to person, all down the truck. I could hear it at first—a soft, hissing sound—until it was drowned out by the noise of the train starting up and beginning to move.

We were on our way to France.

I put my eye to the peephole again, but I couldn't see anything except darkness rushing past so I closed my eyes and leaned back into the corner. For twenty minutes—maybe more—there was no sound except the steady roar of the train, echoing off the walls of the tunnel.

And then there was a jolt and the train stopped.

'What's happened?' said a woman's voice. 'Are we there?'

I couldn't see anything through my peephole except the same darkness as before—only now it wasn't moving. 'Don't think so,' I said.

'We're stuck,' said another voice. 'Stuck in the tunnel—with all that water on top of us! What's going to happen if we don't move? The air—'

'Sssh!' said half a dozen other voices.

But it was too late to stop the feeling of panic that ran through the truck. Justin shifted Taco sideways and put an arm round my shoulders. 'Don't worry,' he whispered. 'Bob knows what he's doing. Everything's going to be fine.'

I pushed away the pictures that came crawling into my mind—wishing I'd never seen *Titanic*. After a moment, I tried looking through the hole again and this time I could see streaks of light. Were they moving?

'Hey!' I shouted. '*Hey!*'

Then there were footsteps, running along the floor of the truck, and Bob's voice came back, right next to my ear. 'Hang on. Let's get you out of there.'

Everyone started calling out to him, but he ignored all the questions and began to unbuckle the side of the truck. Then it began rolling open—and people went beserk all round us.

Half a dozen men jumped up, swinging their bags. They leapt towards the opening, treading on everyone in the way and bursting through the curtain. I heard their feet thud as they jumped down on to the floor of the freight car and I saw the first few slide between the bars at the sides, letting themselves down into the tunnel. Then other people followed them, crowding into the opening and blocking my view.

'What are they doing?' I said. 'Isn't it dangerous?'

'Of course it's dangerous,' Justin said. 'But what else can we do? The train's been stopped. If we want to go any further, we'll have to walk.'

That's what people were doing. Peering between the jumping legs I saw hundreds of them flooding past

58

us. They stumbled along the side of the track, heaving their bags and bundles with them. Their voices echoed off the walls and their torches laced the darkness with tiny, flickering lights.

There were *hundreds* of people. Thousands.

One man saw me peering out of the truck and he shouted up at me. 'You want to get out of there, lad! Before they send the train back to England!'

I pulled on my backpack. 'We've got to go!' I said. And I reached for the bike.

Justin shook his head at me. 'Don't be silly. You can't take *that*!'

'Yes I can!' He was mistaken if he thought I was going to leave it behind. I jumped out of the truck and reached up to lift it down after me.

Justin bent down and caught at my shoulder. 'Wait for us! We mustn't get separated. Hang on to Taco while I get the big rucksack.' He leaned out of the truck and lowered Taco into my arms. 'We'll have to leave the other bags behind.'

'Not mine!' Taco wailed. 'My shoebox is in there!'

'For heaven's sake!' Justin said. But he grabbed Taco's little backpack and threw it out of the truck. 'You take it, Matt. I need to carry Taco.'

He slid down to join us and pulled the rucksack after him. Then he peered nervously down from the freight car. There was only a narrow corridor between the track and the wall and it was jammed with desperate people, all shouting and pushing at each other.

We have to go now! I thought. *Or we'll never get out!*

But Justin wouldn't be hustled. 'I'll go first,' he said slowly. 'Then you hand Taco down to me. You'll have to manage the bike on your own—if you *must* bring it.'

'I must,' I said.

Justin lowered himself down from the freight car, hanging on to the bars so he wouldn't get swept away by the crowd. He held up his free arm and I lifted Taco into it. Then I picked up Taco's little backpack and hung it over my handlebars.

'*Please* don't bring the bike!' Justin called.

I ignored him. 'Get out of the way! It's coming down!'

I tried to push it between the bars too fast and the pedals snagged. When I crouched down, to work them free, the bike and I fell through the gap together and I landed on top of it, wrenching my shoulder and skinning both my knees. It was a struggle to get back on my feet, because people walked straight over me.

By the time I managed to stand up, Justin and Taco had gone—forced away by the weight of the crowd. Justin was looking back and shouting for me to follow, but he couldn't stand still and wait.

I heaved the bike upright and started forward, using it as a battering ram. I was desperate to catch them, but it was impossible to hurry. People kept jumping down from the other freight cars, knocking me sideways and tangling with the wheels of the bike. I was hit by buggies and bags and nearly knocked out by one old man's suitcase.

But I kept going. Every time a space opened up in front of me, I charged through it, keeping my eyes fixed on Justin's head. And he was watching me too, hanging back whenever he got the chance.

When I finally caught up, Justin shifted Taco on to his hip and reached out to grab me. 'Thank goodness!' he said, in a voice I'd never heard before. 'Hang on to my coat—and don't let go, whatever you do.'

'How far is it?' I said. 'How long till we're out of the tunnel?' I couldn't see anything beyond the people in front of me.

But Taco was higher than I was. He reared up in Justin's arms and pointed ahead. 'It's there! I can see the end of the tunnel! There's France!'

'Come on!' Justin shouted. He shoved forward again and somehow I managed to push the bike *and* hold on to his coat. Taco wound his fingers into my hair, yanking on it to make sure I kept up.

It was hard to stay upright with both my hands full and a heavy pack on my back. The crowd behind us kept surging forwards and I was terrified of losing my balance. If I went over again—that would be it. The feet behind would go straight over me and this time I might not get up.

Better not to think about that. Better just to keep going.

We were knocked this way and that, jostled and pushed and barged. Sometimes we staggered forward. Sometimes we came to a sharp stop—and everyone behind crashed into us. Twice I nearly lost Taco's bag and I had to bend down quickly, to catch it before it hit the ground, with Taco shrieking in my ear because he thought the trampling feet were going to flatten his precious shoebox.

It felt as though we were going to be there for ever, struggling through the darkness with our bodies braced against the pressure from behind and the crowd blocking the way ahead. All we could do was shuffle one step after another, on and on and on—

Until suddenly all the pressure disappeared and we burst out of the tunnel into a wide, bright space.

Floodlights blazed down at us from all directions and a voice blared from a loudspeaker, so distorted that I couldn't make out what it was saying. I was deafened and dazzled and caught off balance, so that I almost fell over.

It was raining hard and the wet railway lines gleamed under the floodlights, stretching away in front of us. *What do we do now?* I thought. *Where do we go?*

Taco was still clinging on to my hair and suddenly he started pulling at it, giving it strange little tweaks.

'Stop that!' I said.

But he didn't stop. I reached up, to knock his hand away, and I realized he wasn't doing it on purpose. His whole body was shaking. He was gazing up at the top of the cutting, at the shapes that moved in the darkness beyond the floodlights. And he was terrified.

All along the top of the cutting, on both sides, was a line of crowd barriers. And from behind the barriers, soldiers were staring down at us.

Men with shields and helmets and guns.

6

WE WERE SURROUNDED. Now that my eyes were used to the floodlights, I could see barriers ahead as well. With a solid wall of army vehicles behind them, stretching right across the cutting.

'Where can we go?' I said.

Justin shook his head. 'There isn't anywhere. Except back into the tunnel.'

'I don't want to go back in there,' Taco said plaintively. The rain had already soaked through his fleece and he looked very small and thin with the cloth clinging round his body. Justin tried to put him down, but he clung like a little monkey, closing his eyes and butting his head into Justin's shoulder.

We weren't being pushed and hassled now, but we were still in the middle of a crowd. All round us, people were wandering about, slipping on the wet rails and looking bewildered. Some of them headed for the soldiers at the far end of the cutting. Others ducked back into the tunnel, to escape the rain.

'If we stand here, we'll just get wetter and wetter,' I said. 'What are we going to *do*?'

Justin shook his head again. 'I don't know, Matt.'

'You *must* know,' I said.

'How?' Justin snapped. 'How can I decide what to do, when I haven't got a clue what's happening?'

His voice was so sharp that Taco started crying. Justin sounded desperate and the horrible cut on his face must have got knocked in the tunnel. It was bleeding again and long trickles of red were running down his cheek and into Taco's hair.

Suppose Justin's not all right? I thought. *Who's going to look after us?*

For a moment I was scared too. Then Justin got a grip. 'I'm sorry, Matt,' he said. 'I'll try and find out what's going on in a minute. But the first thing we have to do is keep dry. Can you get our cagoules out?'

He turned round to let me open the rucksack. The cagoules were right there on top, all wrapped up in a big polythene sheet. Not just ours, but Mum's and Grandma Grace's as well.

'We could make a sort of tent,' I said. 'That would keep everything dry.'

Justin glanced up and down the cutting. Other people were settling down around us, making awkward, uncomfortable little camps between the railway tracks. 'OK,' he said. 'Good idea.'

We put on our own cagoules and I laid the two spares on the ground, for us to sit on. Then I made a wall with the luggage and the bike and pulled the polythene sheet over the top, tucking it in all round us. It wasn't much of a tent, but it kept off the wind and most of the rain. Justin and I put Taco in between us, right in the middle, and gradually he began to warm up.

We huddled there for a couple of hours and gradually the sky got lighter and the rain tailed off. But nothing *happened*. The soldiers were still looking down at us, and we were still in the middle of the crowd, stuck under the floodlights in the railway cutting.

People kept trekking up and down the cutting, to talk to the soldiers. But they didn't find out any news. That was obvious from their disappointed faces and the way their shoulders drooped when they came back. It felt as though nothing was ever going to happen, as though the night would never end.

Then, at six o'clock in the morning, Justin's phone started ringing.

'It's Mum!' Taco said excitedly. 'It's got to be Mum!'

It was. We were all so close together that Taco and I could hear her voice too. She started talking the moment Justin answered, asking a stream of frantic questions.

'What's going on? Are you in that terrible place they keep showing on the News? Are you all *right*?'

'What terrible place?' Justin said.

'For heaven's sake!' Mum screeched. 'That dreadful cutting at the end of the tunnel, of course. They're saying there are ten thousand people all penned in together and the pictures are horrific. I keep looking, but I can't see you.'

'It's all *right*,' Justin said. He took a long breath as if he was gathering his strength. When he spoke again, he sounded totally calm. We might have been sitting in a café somewhere, instead of crouching on railway lines in the pouring rain. 'The cutting's not as bad as it looks. Matt's made us a tent.'

'Well done, Matty!' Mum said. 'That's what Grandpa would have done.' I thought she was going to cry. 'But what about food and—'

I missed the next bit, because Taco leaned over the phone and shouted, 'Mum! Mum!' And by the time Justin managed to shut him up, Mum was talking about something else.

'Listen—this is really important,' she said. 'The French Government's going to send most people straight back to England. You can only stay if you've got children *and if your lives have been in danger*. Tell them about the raiders, Justin. And show them your face. How is it?'

Justin touched his cheek. 'It's fine. Just bleeding a bit. But what about you? How—?'

'Bleeding's *good*!' Mum said fiercely. 'I hope it looks really bad. Make sure you tell them how it happened. No—make *Taco* tell them. They'll believe what he says. You've *got* to make sure they let you stay.'

'We will,' said Justin. 'Don't worry. We'll be fine, Ali.' The loudspeaker started up again and he put a hand over his other ear to shut out the noise. 'How's Grace? When can you get here?'

'Not for a while,' said Mum. Suddenly all the energy went out of her voice. 'She's broken her hip and they don't know when they can operate. So we're stuck here—'

'No!' Taco shouted. He leaned over, pushing his face in between Justin and the phone. 'No! You've got to come *now*, Mum!' We tried to shut him up, but it was no use. He went on and on shouting, working himself into a frenzy.

Justin kept trying to talk to Mum, but it was hopeless. In the end he gave up. 'It's no use, Ali,' he shouted, above Taco's shrieks. 'We're just wasting the battery. I'll call you back soon, darling. OK? And—be careful.'

Mum made a funny little noise at the other end and then she was gone. Justin slipped the phone into his back pocket—and Taco screamed even louder, choking and gasping for breath. Justin rocked him and stroked his back, but that didn't help. Nothing would make him stop.

Until Bob appeared.

He came walking down between the railway lines, with his hands in his pockets and a bag slung over his shoulder. There was a tall, sulky-looking girl with him, maybe a bit older than me. Water was dripping off the peak of her baseball cap and running down her face, but she didn't seem to notice. She was too busy glowering down at the rails.

I wondered who she was.

When Bob saw us, he grinned and came strolling over. Taco was still yelling and Bob crouched down to look into his face.

'Boo!' he said.

Taco was so surprised he stopped yelling.

'That's better.' Bob pulled a toffee out of his pocket and dropped it into Taco's lap. 'It's wet enough, without all that crying.'

Taco unwrapped the toffee and put it into his mouth. Then he pointed at the girl. 'Who's she?' he said.

'Her?' Bob put his head on one side. 'She's my daughter, of course.' He looked round at the girl. 'Paige, say hello to Justin and Matthew and Thomas.'

'Taco,' Taco said. 'I'm called Taco.'

The girl looked down at him, without smiling. 'That's not a name.'

'Yes it is.' Taco glared at her. 'It's *my* name. I'm called Taco Bannister.'

Justin gave the girl an apologetic grin. 'He wouldn't eat anything except tacos when he was two, and the name kind of stuck.' He glanced at Bob. 'Didn't know you had a daughter.'

'I'm full of surprises,' Bob said easily. He squatted down, so he could talk to us quietly. 'This is a nice little shelter you've made. But I wouldn't unpack your bags too much. You need to be ready to go when they give the word—if you want a place at the front of the queue.'

Justin sat up. 'Are we moving?'

'Sssh!' Bob waved a hand, to make him lower his voice. 'Not yet. But the soldiers are talking about bringing up some trains to shift us from here. They'll shunt most people straight back to England.'

'*Most* people?' Justin raised one eyebrow.

'People without children.' Bob winked at Taco. 'But people with children can stay. They're sending us into the country. Place called Lemon Dough.'

70

(That's what it sounded like, anyway.)

'What sort of place?' Justin said carefully.

'We'll find out, won't we?' Bob grinned. '*If* we manage to get on the right train. So—be ready.' He was going to move on when something caught his eye. 'Where did you get the bike?'

'It's mine,' I said. 'I brought it in the truck.'

'Did you now?' Bob gave me a sharp look. 'Should have charged you extra.' He ran his eyes over the bike and then glanced up at Paige. 'Hey!' he said. As if he'd just had the idea. 'Why don't you hang out with Matthew and Taco for a while? You can get to know them while Justin and I go for a walk.'

'I don't think I should leave the boys,' Justin said nervously.

Bob waved a hand, brushing that aside. 'They'll be fine with Paige. And they can mind the luggage.' He slipped the bag off his shoulder and pushed it into our shelter. 'Paige is good with children—aren't you, Paige?'

Paige lifted her head and gave him a strange look, as if he wasn't quite human. Then she crouched down and wriggled under the polythene with Taco and me. She bent her long, skinny legs and rested her chin on her knees.

'Got anything to eat?' she said.

You're not having any of our food, I thought. But

she'd started Taco off. The moment she mentioned food, he began to whine.

'Matty, I'm starving. I need some breakfast. *Pleeeease—*'

'Yeah, Matty,' Paige drawled. 'What have you got for breakfast? Where do you keep the food?'

Before I could stop her, she'd reached under the polythene and unlaced my backpack. She pushed her hand inside and pulled out the first thing she found.

'What's this, then? Hey!' And she started to laugh.

It was the bundle of paper Mum had given me when we left home. Now it was light, I could see it properly—and it was *money*. Hundreds of twenty pound notes rolled up together, with a rubber band around them.

'Give that *back*!' I said. I snatched it out of her hand and pushed it right down to the very bottom of the backpack, underneath the tool roll.

That gave her the chance to get at Justin's rucksack. When I looked up, she was rummaging inside, pulling things out and scattering them everywhere.

'What's this? Raw pasta! What use is that? And this—oh, *yuck*!' She dropped Justin's spare boxer shorts into my lap.

'Stop it!' I said. 'What d'you think you're doing?' I tried to pull the bag away from her, but we were all huddled up too close. She dipped her hand in again and pulled out a plastic bag full of pale orange chunks.

'Aha! What's *this?*' she said.

I glared at her. 'It's raw swede.'

Paige started laughing. 'The height of luxury!' she said. She dipped her fingers into the bag and picked out a handful of swede. 'Here, Taco. Breakfast!'

She bit into a piece and I reached over and snatched the bag back from her. 'That's stealing,' I said.

Taco looked at the bag of swede. 'It's wicked to steal food,' he said.

I could tell he wasn't really thinking about Paige. He was remembering the men who'd crashed through our house.

Paige didn't know that, of course. And she didn't care. She took another bite of swede and chewed energetically. 'Yum,' she said. 'Delicious!' And then she said it again, in a silly voice. '*Délicieux!*'

Taco stared at her. 'Is that French?'

'*Bien sûr, mon petit,*' Paige said. 'Aren't you going to have some lovely swede?'

Taco's hand snaked into the bag. He pulled out a lump of swede and slid it into his mouth. I hadn't realized he was that hungry.

'*Bon appetit,*' Paige said in her stupid Frenchy voice. She raised her eyebrows at me. 'What about you?'

I shook my head. 'Not hungry.'

It wasn't true, of course. I was *too* hungry. Once I

started eating I wouldn't be able to stop. If I dipped my hand into that bag of swede, it would be empty in a couple of minutes—and we hadn't got anything else, except the pasta. So I rolled the bag up and pushed it back into the rucksack. Then I fastened the top, very tightly.

Paige swallowed her last mouthful of swede. Then she looked up sharply. 'What's that noise?' she said. She poked her head out of the shelter and glanced up the cutting. 'He-ey! Look!'

I could hear the noise too. Feet slithering on the rails and a lot of voices muttering. Pushing Taco off my lap, I crawled out of the shelter to take a look and saw hundreds of people on the move.

Everywhere around us, people were jumping to their feet and hurrying up the cutting, running between the railway lines and tripping on the sleepers. They were all heading towards the soldiers who were blocking the way ahead. And those who'd already reached the barrier were crowding together, struggling to get to the very front.

'What is it?' I said. 'Do you think we're missing something?'

Paige frowned. 'I don't know. But we can't go off and leave all this stuff.' She peered forward, shading her eyes with her hand. 'Where are those two men?'

For a moment I couldn't think what she was talking

about. Then I realized she meant Bob and Justin. 'They were there right at the beginning,' I said. 'So they must be in the middle of the crowd.'

'No they're not,' Paige said suddenly. '*There* they are!' And she pointed up the cutting.

Bob and Justin were coming the opposite way, heading out of the crowd towards us. They must have been right at the front. Each of them was carrying a bottle of water and a couple of long French loaves.

Bob knew, I thought. *He knew what was going to happen.* He and Justin looked very pleased with themselves. When they reached us, they were laughing and swiping at each other with the loaves.

'They're not exactly fresh,' Bob said cheerfully. 'Must have been made days ago. But it's food and it's free, so no moaning.'

He snapped the loaves into pieces, breaking them over his knee. Then he handed the pieces out and we all squeezed under the polythene and started to eat. The bread was as hard as iron, but we chewed away at it until we'd eaten every crumb. Because Bob was right—it was food. And we were starving hungry.

When it was all finished, Taco wiped his hands on his trousers. Then he looked up at Justin. 'Can we phone Mum again?' he said.

Justin hesitated. 'We ought to save the battery,' he

said slowly. 'I don't know how we're going to charge it if it goes flat.'

Taco pulled a face. 'But you promised. You said we'd phone her back.'

'That's true,' Justin said. 'All right—but just a short call. And no crying. Promise?'

'Promise,' Taco said.

Justin reached round into his back pocket—and suddenly his face changed. He stood up quickly and felt in the pocket again. 'It's not there,' he said. 'It's gone.'

He went down on his knees and started fumbling around the shelter, but there was nothing there either.

'It must have fallen out of your pocket,' Bob said. 'When all those people were jostling us. Or—'

Justin didn't wait to hear what the 'or' was. He went racing up the cutting to hunt for his phone in the middle of the crowd. And after a while we saw him walking back, very slowly, studying every inch of the ground.

But he never found it.

7

WE WERE IN that cutting for another *twenty-four hours*. And for most of that time it was raining.

We'd been lucky to get some of the water the soldiers were handing out. They hadn't had enough for everyone and some people started getting desperate. They held out mugs and polythene bags to try and collect the rainwater, but they only managed to catch an inch or so—and they got soaked to the skin while they were doing it.

After the first night, Bob gathered a group of people together and they all went up to the soldiers, to ask if they could rig us up some kind of shelter.

But it was useless.

'They wouldn't talk to us,' Bob said when he came back. 'Just kept pointing at the train in the tunnel. They'd like everyone to get back on board—so they can ship us all home again.'

'Well we're not going!' said one of the women from his group. 'Their government's promised we could stay and I'm staying. I'm not taking Charlotte back to England.'

The woman's name was Muriel and she was small and fierce. She was wearing combat trousers and heavy boots, with a rucksack on her back and a baby strapped to her front. When the rest of the group drifted away, she took off her rucksack and sat down next to our shelter.

'We ought to stick together,' she said.

She pulled the baby out of its carrier and started feeding it. It was like her—small and pink-faced, with short hair and a loud voice. When the guzzling stopped, Muriel looked round at us all.

'Anyone want to hold Charlotte?' she said.

Paige leaned back and closed her eyes and I pretended I hadn't heard. I don't mind mess as long as it's oil and mud and grease. But babies? Yuck!

'I'll hold her,' Taco said.

Muriel dumped the baby on his lap and he started pulling faces at her and making silly noises.

At least it stopped him asking for food and phone calls.

That afternoon, the soldiers came down the cutting, handing out forms to everyone. The forms were in French.

'Hey!' Muriel shouted. She flapped her paper at the soldier who'd given it to her. 'What am I supposed to do with this? Haven't you got them in English?'

The soldier shook his head at her, said something very fast and moved on to the next group of people. Muriel was outraged. She jumped up and shouted after him.

'What's that supposed to mean? Why can't someone *explain?*'

Paige opened her eyes a crack. 'He told you the forms are applications for asylum,' she said wearily. 'They're in French because that's the rules. We have to answer the questions in French too.'

We all turned round and stared at her.

'How come you understood him?' I said.

'Let me see.' Paige frowned sarcastically. 'How *did* I understand? Hm'm. Could it possibly be—because I *speak French?*'

'But you're English,' Taco said.

'Only half English.' Paige shrugged. 'My mother's French.' She looked up at Bob with an odd little smile. 'Isn't she?'

Bob looked down at her. 'I'm counting on you to fill in our form,' he said quickly. 'You can help other people too. Muriel would like a hand with hers—wouldn't you, Muriel?'

'We-ell, I *would*, but—' Muriel hesitated. 'I might need to write about some pretty unpleasant things. Paige is a bit young for all that.'

'She'll be fine,' Bob said firmly. He took a pen from his pocket and held it out to Paige. 'Why don't you make a start? Shall we do ours first?'

'With everyone listening?' Paige raised her eyebrows. 'Don't you want some privacy?'

'Everyone's going to want privacy.' Bob looked at the people clustered around us. 'If you give Paige and me some space to fill in our form, she'll help you with yours afterwards. Right?'

Paige sat up sharply. For a moment I thought she was going to argue, but then she shrugged and started reading the form, ignoring the rest of us. We shuffled out of the way and soon she and Bob were sitting in the middle of an empty, private space.

As private as you can be, surrounded by thousands of people.

For a couple of minutes I watched them sitting with their heads together, discussing the form. Then Justin leaned towards me.

'When I talk to Paige about our form, keep Taco out of the way,' he said softly. 'I don't want him hearing the stuff I'll need to say.'

'What about me?' I said. 'If Paige can hear it, why can't I? I'm not a baby.'

Justin frowned. 'I can't worry about Paige. My job's looking after you and Taco. And I don't want you there. Promise?'

I didn't like it, but I promised. And when our turn came round, I caught hold of Taco's hand, to stop him going to sit with Paige.

'You don't want to listen to all that French stuff,' I said. 'Stay here and I'll tell you a story.'

He looked at me warily. 'What kind of story?'

'Spiderman,' I said. That was always a winner.

'Spiderman with *dinosaurs*?'

'OK. With dinosaurs.' I wasn't sure how I was going to get them in, but I'd have to manage it somehow.

'*And* a polar bear?'

I started with that. 'One day, up in the Arctic, a polar bear was catching fish when suddenly—'

It wasn't a very good story. I couldn't concentrate on the polar bear, because I was watching Justin and Paige over the top of Taco's head. Justin was talking steadily, staring down at his hands and Paige was sitting cross-legged, very still and upright. She looked exhausted, but she was listening carefully. And every now and then she leaned forward and wrote something on the form, making letters with sharp little jabs of the pen.

She was still writing when Spiderman and the dinosaurs defeated the evil polar bear. By that time the sky was dark and Taco was falling asleep with his head in my lap. I made him as comfortable as I could and then closed my eyes . . .

At four in the morning, Bob came to wake us up. 'Time to pack,' he whispered to Justin. 'They'll be walking us down to the trains in an hour or so. Keep it quiet if you want to get ahead.'

Taco half-opened his eyes. 'Why can't they bring the trains here?' he mumbled.

'And electrocute us all?' Bob said. 'A little walk won't hurt you anyway. We'll be riding soon enough.'

Paige was rubbing her eyes and pulling on her baseball cap. She stood and watched while we took our shelter to bits and packed up the pieces. Muriel woke up too and when we set off up the cutting she was right behind us.

We had to wait for a couple of hours at the barrier before the soldiers would let us through. But as soon as it was light they started moving us on, marshalling us into a long, straggling line. It was awkward walking on the track and Taco was struggling, so I let him ride on the bike for most of the way. I had to keep my arm tight round his waist to stop him falling off as it bumped over the sleepers.

Paige was just ahead of us, dragging along with her head down. She looked exhausted, but Taco leaned forward and called out to her.

'Hey! Paige! Will you teach me French?'

She looked back over her shoulder and rattled off a stream of words in a flat, bored voice. '*Un, deux, trois, quatre, cinq, six, sept, huit, neuf, dix.*'

Nothing clever about that. Anyone can count up to ten in French. But Taco thought it was fantastic. '*Un der trah—*' he started. 'Oh, I can't remember it all. Tell me again. *Slower.*'

I smacked his arm. 'Leave Paige alone. You don't need to know that stuff. You're English.'

I was only trying to be kind, but Paige took it the wrong way. She dropped back, so she was walking next to Taco, and started teaching him the numbers properly. Saying them over and over again. And again. And again. I thought she was doing it just to annoy me.

It was light by the time we reached the station and there were two trains waiting for us. Both very long. We hadn't seen much of Bob on the way there, because he'd been wandering up and down the line, talking to all sorts of people. But he reappeared suddenly and caught hold of Paige's arm.

'We need to stick together,' he said. 'This is where they split us up.'

The soldiers were herding people on to the platforms, sending some one way and some another. I didn't understand what was happening until we reached the front of the line—and suddenly it was obvious.

People with children went on the left-hand train. Everyone else was herded on to the other one.

There was a lot of noise and shoving as people argued with the soldiers, shouting at them to change their minds.

'What's the matter?' Taco said. 'Why are those people being so *rude*?'

'Sssh!' Justin looked round anxiously. 'They're upset because they can't stay here. They have to go back through the tunnel.'

The soldiers waved us through to the left-hand train without even looking at our papers. But they nearly made a mistake with Muriel. She was right behind us, so loaded down with bags that they didn't realize the one on her front was a baby carrier. They tried to push her the other way, on to the train that was going back to England.

'Are you blind?' Muriel yelled. 'Can't you see I've got a child? *Look!* There's no way I'm taking her back!'

The soldiers prodded at the baby carrier, as if they didn't believe her—which woke Charlotte up. When she started screaming too, they finally gave in and let Muriel get on with us. As she hauled herself on to the train, she was shaking all over and muttering under her breath.

'They're not even looking properly. Don't they *care?*'

Inside the train it was like a wrestling match. People didn't want to let go of any of their luggage, because they were afraid of losing it. So they were squeezing into the seats with all their bags, fighting for space to keep everything together.

I thought I'd have to leave the bike in the space at the end of the coach, but Bob shook his head when he saw me take out the padlock. 'You don't want to lose sight of it,' he said. 'Anyone with a hacksaw could cut through that little chain.'

He picked up the bike and hoisted it over his head, launching himself down the carriage. Somehow he managed to manoeuvre the bike over people's heads and round their suitcases, bellowing out a constant stream of cheerful warnings.

'Mind your backs there! Watch out for low-flying cyclists, Tom! Hey, Muriel, don't let that baby chew the tyres! And if you kids could just breathe in a bit . . . '

He seemed to know half the people in the carriage and most of them ducked out of the way without even grumbling—even when he hoisted the bike on to a table and settled it there, up against the window.

'Come on,' he called back to me. 'If you and Paige sit on opposite sides you can hold it here. Then it won't be taking up any room.'

Somehow we managed to squeeze ourselves in and Justin sat down next to me, with Taco on his lap. Bob ushered Muriel into the seat beside Paige. Then he packed our bags on to the rack—and on to the table and into all the spaces around us.

'That's you sorted,' he said cheerfully. And he disappeared down the carriage to help someone else with a baby.

More and more people kept squeezing in. Soon they were standing all down the carriage, holding their children or perching them on top of heaps of bags. It got hotter and hotter and it was impossible to move. And the train didn't start for another two hours.

But no one complained—because we knew we were the lucky ones.

We were going to Lemon Dough—wherever that was.

8

WHEN WE FINALLY did start, it was a slow, slow journey. And *boring*. There was nothing much to see and we kept stopping to let other trains pass. After an hour or so, I actually fell asleep, in spite of the bike and the way we were crammed in.

When I woke up, the sun was beginning to set, and we were stopped in the middle of nowhere. *Fields*, I thought. *And cows. And trees. BORING.*

But there was something else too. Bob was leaning over the table, peering through the bike frame.

Just there, a road ran close to the railway line. In between us and the road, on a piece of scrubby waste ground, was a little group of tents. Not a proper campsite. Just half a dozen pop-up tents huddled together, with cars parked beside them. Someone had strung up a washing line between two trees and it was heavy with wet clothes dripping on to the grass.

I yawned. 'That's a weird place to camp.'

'They're not on holiday,' Bob said. As if I should have guessed. 'Look—it's all British cars.'

Two little girls—about Taco's age—came out of one of the tents and started chasing each other up and down the verge. They were only wearing vests and pants and their arms and legs were as thin as sticks. Muriel shivered and cuddled Charlotte tighter as the train started again.

Ten minutes later there was another hold-up. Not in a station—we always rattled through those—but in the middle of nowhere.

'Why don't we just get out here?' Muriel said wearily. She was having trouble keeping Charlotte on her lap because she was wriggling so much. 'We could disappear into the countryside and look after ourselves.'

'No we couldn't.' Bob shook his head. 'All the doors are locked. They don't want to lose us before we get to Lemon Dough.'

It was another four hours before we finally stopped in a station. It was pitch dark by then, and the soldiers wouldn't let us get off the train. We had to stay where we were, jammed into our smelly, noisy carriage, until the sky turned pink and the sun started coming up.

As it began to get light, people crowded towards the windows, to see where we'd landed up. *Les Mondeaux*, said the name board on the platform. It looked as if we were on the edge of a small town. Houses straggled along beside the railway line and up the slope beyond. A wide street, lined with trees, led up to a dark, ugly church at the top of the hill.

There was nothing moving. No people. No cars. The whole town was silent and still.

At last the soldiers decided it was light enough to let us off the train. By then, most of us were too stiff to move and all the little children were asleep again. They didn't like being woken up, so there was lots of screaming and it got worse when the bags started crashing around.

We had to wait until the carriage was half empty before we could pull our bags down and lift the bike off the table. And it was much, much longer before we finally inched down the aisle and on to the platform. As soon as we stepped off the train, the soldiers started hassling us. They didn't want us hanging around in the station. *Lemon Dough*, they kept saying, pointing out of the station and up through the town.

We joined the line of people trailing up the main street, shuffling along between lines of soldiers. They were watching us, all the time—but they needn't have bothered. None of us knew where we were. All we

89

could do was go where they sent us, plodding slowly up the hill.

By that time, people had started coming out of their houses. As we trudged past they stopped to stare at us. Old women with shopping bags. Kids on their way to school. Smart young couples in cars. They watched us walk by, but no one said anything to us. No one even smiled.

Taco pulled at my coat. 'What are they doing?' he whispered. 'I don't like it.'

'They don't look very happy to see us, do they?' Bob grinned down at him. 'I reckon we need a bit of PR.' He looked at the line of people ahead of us and gave me a nudge. 'See that woman in front? The one with three toddlers?'

How could I miss her? She was older than most other people and she kept stopping and holding everything up because the children were whining round her legs. They all wanted to be carried at once.

'What a pain,' I said.

Bob looked at my bike. 'Reckon you could get a couple of the kids on there? That would really help her.' He slipped my bag off the handlebars and on to his own shoulder. Then he planted his hand in the middle of my back and gave me a push. 'Let's go,' he said.

He pushed me forward, towards the woman, and when we caught up he tapped her on the arm. 'Looks like you need a bit of help,' he said. 'How about putting two of your kids on the bike?'

She looked round and I thought she was going to hug him. 'That would be wonderful!' Her face was grey and exhausted.

The children liked the idea as well. They all started shouting at once.

'I want to ride the bike, Granny.'

'No! Me, Granny Kara! Me!'

'*Me!*'

Bob picked up the biggest boy and dumped him on the saddle. Then he lifted the middle one on to the handlebars.

'You'll have to hold on to that one,' the woman said. 'He wriggles.' She scooped up the smallest child and sat him on her hip. 'Now we can really get going!'

She strode off and the two kids on the bike started shouting to follow her. The one on the handlebars grabbed at my neck and the other flung his arms round my waist. They almost throttled me and the bike lurched sideways, so all their weight was against my chest.

I was just going to tell Bob I couldn't manage them both—when an old man stepped out of a shop and lumbered towards us.

He was wearing a grubby old cap and carrying a couple of long loaves under his arm. He broke bits off one of the loaves and gave them to the kids on the bike. Then he patted my shoulder and rattled off something in French.

I didn't understand a word, but I heard Paige laugh behind me. As soon as the old man tottered off, I looked round at her.

'What was all that about?' I said.

She grinned sarcastically. 'He said you were a good little boy.' She looked at the kids on the bike and laughed again.

I'd rather have had a piece of bread.

After that, I couldn't throw the kids off the bike. So I took them all the way up the hill—and I realized Bob was right. It *was* good PR. Some of the people watching us started to smile and a couple of women patted me on the arm.

But no one brought any more bread.

At the top of the hill was an ugly church, with a little square in front of it. Beyond the square, the street bent round, between stone buildings, and then plunged down the other side of the hill. Suddenly the countryside opened out in front of us. At the bottom of the hill the houses ended and the farmland began.

And there, on the very edge of the town, was a big, brick building, with three or four football pitches beside it and open fields beyond. At least, the fields *should* have been open. But they weren't. And there was no chance of playing anything on the football pitches.

All the ground round the building was covered in tents. Not little pop-ups, like the ones we'd seen from the train, but blue tunnel tents—hundreds and hundreds of them, pitched in long, straight rows. And in among the tents there were rough little shelters, made of corrugated iron and cardboard and polythene.

Looking down from the top of the hill we could see it all. The early morning light glinted on metal and wet mud, and filtered through the smoke that came drifting up towards us. There was a twitter of distant voices, rising and falling, and the air smelt of ashes and disinfectant.

Even though it was early, people were moving around. From the top of the hill they looked tired and aimless, trailing in all directions across the crowded fields. We could see the bare, brown paths their feet had worn between the tents.

As soon as we saw it, we all knew that was where we were being sent. The only place where there would be food and shelter. Even though it looked full already, we would have to fit in somehow and find a way of living there.

Because that was Lemon Dough.

We couldn't just walk in. First of all we had to be registered. And that meant spending the whole day in another long queue.

It started at the gates of the camp and stretched right up to the top of the hill. The soldiers chivvied us off the tarmac and made us stand on the grass verge beside the road. It was still raining and there was no shelter, but they kept us standing there for hours.

Snippets of news kept drifting up from the front of the queue. *They're going to give us tents . . . food vouchers . . . after we're registered . . .* But there was nothing to eat or drink while we were waiting. All we could do was shuffle slowly down the hill, towards those gates.

After ten minutes, Taco was totally bored. He was starting to whine when Paige said, 'How about learning some more French? We could do the days of the week. *Lundi, mardi . . .* '

Taco loved that, of course, but I couldn't see the point. Lemon Dough was for English people—and we weren't going to be there for long anyway. Just until things calmed down at home. I turned my back on them both and stared back up at the town, wondering how big it was and if there was food in the shops.

I wish I'd kept my eyes on the road instead.

I didn't look round when I heard the tractor coming up the hill behind me. So I didn't see the big, wide trailer it was pulling. It was some kind of farm machinery that stuck out on either side of the tractor, almost to the edge of the verge. That would have been all right except that, just as the tractor drew level with us, a car came over the hill, speeding up as it left the town. It was driving carelessly, almost in the middle of the road.

Suddenly it came face to face with the tractor and both the drivers swerved, automatically. The tractor swung out to the side of the road, up against the verge.

'Watch out!' shouted someone below us.

Justin caught my arm and pulled me away, seconds before the corner of the trailer scraped across the place where I'd been standing. He saved me from being hurt—but he did it so fast that I let go of the bike. It crashed to the ground—right in the path of that sharp, heavy corner.

The metal graunched across the front wheel and *ping! ping! ping!* I heard half a dozen spokes snap. I don't think the driver knew what he'd done. He went on up the hill without even turning round to look. Leaving me gazing at the wreckage.

It could have been worse. The tractor might have run over the rim and ruined the wheel completely. It might have crashed into the frame and trashed the whole bike. As it was, I'd just lost a handful of spokes (six, to be exact) and spokes can be replaced.

Except—how was I going to find any here? And even if I found some, where would I get the money to pay for them?

Just at that moment, the queue began to shuffle forward. I picked up the bike and tried to wheel it along with me, but the broken spokes stuck out jaggedly, tangling against the others and catching on people's legs.

There was no time to remove them. I pulled the laces out of my trainers and tied the broken spokes up to the good spokes, as best I could. Then I lifted the front wheel off the ground and moved forward with everyone else.

Better not to think about it. Not until I could have a proper look.

By the time we reached the front of the queue, it was well into the afternoon. We inched through the gates and at last—half an hour later—we finally made it into the brick building at the top of the camp.

It had obviously started out as a sports centre, like the one where Justin used to play badminton.

The front door took us into a reception area, with a corridor opening off it. I could see a couple of squash courts and some changing rooms and there was a big hall with wall bars, and white lines on the floor.

But this sports centre was different, because people were *living* in all those spaces.

The whole building was jammed with them. Little family groups, sitting on blankets, with their possessions heaped up around them. There was a lot of noise—talking, arguing, even a bit of laughter—but that wasn't too bad. The people who worried me were the ones who weren't doing anything. Who were just sitting still, staring into nowhere.

I didn't like that.

Even though we were inside, we still had more waiting to do. The queue stretched across the reception area to the counter at the far end, where they were registering us all.

There were four women sitting behind the counter. Two of them were asking questions and the other two were entering the answers on to a computer. They all looked pale and frazzled, as though they hadn't slept for days.

There were two men hanging around as well, but I couldn't work out what they were supposed to be doing, because they were busy having a row. They both had huge great bags under their eyes and half an inch of stubble on their chins.

And everyone was shouting. The men were yelling because they were having an argument. The women asking questions were trying to make themselves heard. And the women on the computers kept asking for everything to be repeated because they couldn't hear.

The whole place was crackling with tension. It felt like sitting on a box of fireworks, with a match fizzling next to it. Everyone in the queue was tired already and now they were starting to get angry.

Muriel was the worst. She was standing behind me and I could hear her muttering about all the delay, fizzing like a rocket that was ready to explode. And every time someone behind pushed her forward, her knees bashed into the back wheel of my bike.

The fourth time it happened, she started snapping at me. 'Can't you keep that thing out of my way? What's it doing in here anyway? This isn't a *garage*!'

She was so fierce I didn't know what to say. And Taco gave her a long look and burst into tears.

'Oh, I'm *sorry*,' Muriel said. 'I don't know what's happening to me. I used to be quite a nice person. Here.' She fumbled in her pocket, as if she was going to give Taco a present. But all she could find was one small, squashed raisin. A bit dusty.

She held it out, apologetically, and Taco took it and put it straight in his mouth. He started sucking it, very slowly—and suddenly I couldn't stop staring at him. I was hypnotized by his mouth. By the way it moved every time he turned the raisin over with his tongue.

It was days since I'd had anything to eat, apart from bread and water and a few mouthfuls of raw swede. Now Taco had a whole, sweet, juicy raisin. I wanted that raisin so much I could hardly breathe. I kept imagining how it would feel in my mouth, with its tough, wrinkled skin and the sweet, juicy flesh inside.

It was a relief when Taco finally gave up and swallowed it.

Bob and Paige were immediately in front of us in the queue. As they reached the counter, Bob whispered something in Paige's ear and gave her a little push. And she stepped up to the desk—and *smiled*.

Then she started talking in French—and the woman behind the counter smiled back at her. *Bernadette* said her name badge. I don't think she was French, but she looked easier when she heard Paige speaking it. I felt the whole queue behind me relax. And Taco was staring at Paige with his eyes wide and his mouth hanging open, as if she was some kind of genius.

She didn't *have* to speak French. The Bernadette woman talked perfectly good English—I'd been listening to her for half an hour. But the French made everything go much more smoothly. Even though Paige had to translate for Bob, they were finished twice as fast as everyone else.

Bernadette rubber-stamped a piece of paper and handed it over to Bob. Then she beckoned to one of the men to take them through into the camp.

'Hang on,' Bob said cheerfully. 'We'll wait for our friends.' He beckoned us forward. 'Your turn.'

For a second, Bernadette's smile disappeared. She obviously didn't like having her system disrupted. But then she noticed Justin's cheek, and suddenly her face changed and she beckoned too.

That wasn't really surprising. The wound was still swollen and cockled up where they'd stitched it, and in the last twenty-four hours that whole side of his face had turned blue and yellow and purple—with an ugly jagged scab zigzagging right across it. It looked horrible—and she wanted to know why.

Bob leaned towards Justin. 'Lay it on thick,' he muttered. 'Especially about the children being there when it happened. That should make sure they don't send you back.'

Justin stepped up to the counter. 'Good evening,' he said politely.

Bernadette nodded. 'Good evening,' she said. And then, 'Your face—'

Justin took a deep breath. 'We were raided,' he began, 'more than once. The raiders took our food—of course—but that wasn't the worst. They . . . '

Taco put his hands over his ears and butted his head into my chest. I wrapped my arms round him, shutting out the sound. But no one shut it out for me. I had to listen as Justin kept on talking.

' . . . the second time there were more of them. They had guns, and . . . '

Taco started to shiver. I pulled his head inside my coat and shut my eyes. Closed my ears against Justin's voice.

Then Bob touched my arm. 'It's OK, Matt. He's finished. We can go into the camp.'

I unwrapped Taco's head and let Justin pick him up. Then we followed one of the grumpy, unshaven men through the door beside the counter.

9

WE WENT INTO a room stacked with wooden boxes and piles of white plastic buckets. The man doled out buckets to Bob and Justin, taking the lid off one, to show us they were full of other things like saucepans and mugs. Then he took us through a second door that led outside, into the camp.

There were paving stones round the building, but beyond that everything was bare earth. Someone had laid down a row of empty sacks, to make a pathway, but the mud still squelched up round our shoes.

There was mud *everywhere*.

It was starting to get dark by then, but long queues of people were waiting at the back of the building. They had buckets too, but I didn't really get what was going on until Paige said, 'At least we can get water.'

Then I realized there were taps there and those people were waiting to fill their buckets.

They were going to wait a long time. The queues stretched right down the hill.

At the bottom of the first field, our guide took out a torch and shone it off to the right. 'Toilets!' he said cheerfully.

There was a long row of portaloos lined up against the fence. They had some screening beyond them and the man muttered something in French. Paige pulled a face.

'There aren't enough toilets,' she said. 'But there are trenches behind those screens. We can use those if we need to—but we mustn't go anywhere else.'

'What are trenches?' Taco muttered. 'What does she mean?'

Justin whispered in his ear and the man laughed and led us on down the hill, into the next field. Squelch, squelch, squelch. He was talking away all the time, in a mixture of English and French, and Paige was listening carefully.

Suddenly she stopped dead. '*What?*' she said.

The man gave a take-it-or-leave-it shrug.

Paige turned to us. 'They've run out of tents,' she said furiously. 'They're expecting some more on Friday, but until then we'll have to manage the best we can. He says we can choose a place in the bottom field.'

There was a horrible silence. Then Justin said, 'Well, at least we're in the right place. When the tents do come.'

Bob didn't waste time talking. He pulled out his own torch and shone it round the bottom field. 'Let's go down there,' he said briskly. 'Up against the fence by the road. We can keep an eye on everything from there.'

Paige scowled. 'But it's full of *thistles*.'

'That's why it's not taken already. Come on.' Bob picked up his bag and headed through the gate, picking his way between the tents in the bottom field.

Justin hesitated for a second and then we all trailed after Bob. By the time we reached him, he was already hacking at the thistles. Justin and I pitched in and helped him, trampling down the stalks he'd left.

'I'll go and fetch some water,' Paige said quickly. She grabbed both the buckets and set off up the hill again.

When she came back, Muriel was with her. She dumped the baby carrier on the ground, with Charlotte still in it.

'Keep her happy,' she said to Taco.

She began trampling up and down with Justin and me—and she was much better at it, because of her heavy boots. In ten minutes or so, we'd cleared a patch ten feet wide.

Muriel pulled a big polythene sheet out of her backpack and Justin added the one we'd brought. He and Bob rigged up a rough kind of shelter that was big enough to take us all.

Just about.

It wasn't anything like a tent, but it was all we had. And that was how we passed the rest of the night. Huddled together under a couple of polythene sheets, with no food except raw pasta that we couldn't cook, and only water to drink.

It was the coldest night I've ever spent.

In the morning, Justin did a deal with Bob. He gave him half a cup of our pasta and Bob lent us his phone, to call Mum. For five minutes.

When she heard where we were, she was frantic. 'You mean you're out in the rain? Like *cows*?'

'It's OK,' Justin said. 'We'll get a tent tomorrow.'

'A *tent*?' screeched Mum. 'It's too cold for camping. You need to be inside, in the warm.'

'There isn't anywhere inside,' Justin said. He sounded very tired. 'I'm sorry. There's nothing else we can do.'

Taco wriggled his head in between Justin and the phone. 'We could come home,' he said hopefully.

'No you couldn't.' Mum's voice was definite. 'You'll stay over there until I tell you it's safe to come back. Now—how's Justin's face?'

Justin pushed Taco out of the way before he could answer. 'I'm fine,' he said firmly. 'Almost better now.' He was lying of course, but it was a good lie. No point in worrying Mum. 'And how is—?'

'What about the *boys*?' Mum said, interrupting him. 'Are they all right?'

Taco wriggled up to the phone again. 'I'm learning to speak French! There's this girl called Paige and she's teaching me. Listen!' And he started babbling away in a stupid voice.

I could see Bob looking at his watch, working out how long we'd been. *I have to be careful of the battery*, he'd said. He wouldn't let us have much longer—and Taco was just wasting the call. I tried to get the phone away from him, but he screamed and held on tighter. And suddenly Mum was yelling at me to leave him alone.

I tried to explain, but at that moment two big trucks came rumbling past us, on the road, and a huge shout went up from all over the camp.

'Tents!'

It was so loud that Mum heard it down the phone. 'Quick!' she shouted. 'Make sure you get one!'

Justin snatched the phone back from Taco. 'But you haven't told us—'

'Things are fine!' Mum shrieked. 'Now get in the tent queue!'

'I'll call again soon,' Justin said. 'I love you.' But Mum had already rung off.

Justin handed the phone back to Bob and started running up the hill, with Muriel close behind him.

'Look after Taco,' he called back to me.

'And Charlotte!' shouted Muriel.

I thought Bob would go too, but he didn't. He just sat there grinning.

'Don't you want a tent?' I said.

He laughed. 'Think they're just going to hand them out?' he said. 'So people can take them and pitch them anywhere?'

I didn't get what he meant, but Paige did. She began to laugh too.

'Facing in all directions!' she said. 'With the guy ropes tangled up like knitting!'

Bob looked pleased, as if she was cleverer than he'd expected. 'That's right. They won't let that happen, will they? They'll want to stay in control. I reckon they'll probably pitch the tents in that field down there. And then they'll choose who has them. Wonder how long that will take.'

He strolled away up the hill, without hurrying, and Paige stared after him.

'He's *smart*,' she said. 'Isn't he?'

She sounded as if she'd only just understood that. But everyone knew Bob was a fixer. And she was his *daughter*. How could she not know already?

He was absolutely right, of course. The people who charged up the hill weren't given tents to take away. They were organized into teams to pitch the tents in neat, organized rows. Muriel had to come back, to look after Charlotte, but Justin was working all day.

They put the tents exactly where Bob had predicted, in the third field down from the sports centre. And—just like he said—they chose who was going to move in first. Muriel got one—because of Charlotte.

'Woo-hoo, baby!' she shrieked. 'We've got a new home!'

She slung the baby carrier on her back and began collecting all her bags. I thought she might have left us the polythene sheet, but she pulled it away from our shelter and took it with her.

'Sorry, but I'll need it,' she said.

Bob went up too, to help her carry the bags. And he took Paige with him, so he could talk to the soldiers. When they came back he knew all about the tents.

'We won't get one today. But they're bringing some more tomorrow. In the meantime, here's some food.'

It was more stale bread. Of course.

Justin broke ours into three pieces and held one out to me. The sight of it made me feel sick. I knew just how it would feel in my mouth—hard and dusty at the same time—and the way it would turn to slop if I dipped it in water to make it softer. I was hungry all right, but—

I can't eat any more of that.

Justin saw my face. 'You *must* eat it,' he said. 'Please, Matt. I don't know what I'll do if you get ill.' He pushed the bread into my hand.

It was so hard it actually scratched my fingers. Just looking at it made my tongue feel rough, but I knew he was right. I had to eat it. I *had* to. I braced myself and opened my mouth.

But before I could bite into the bread, a voice said, 'Here—swap you!' It was Muriel, and she was grinning all over her face. She had a piece of bread in her hand too—but hers was *toasted*.

'The stove in the tent is fantastic!' she said. 'I'll toast all the bread if you like.'

That was the first time I ever smelt toast. I mean *really* smelt it. The smell made my mouth water. Every piece of toast I ever ate before was just something to cover with jam or Marmite or peanut butter. But now there was nothing to put on top of it—and it was delicious. It was still hard, of course, but it was *different*. And that made it a feast.

We gave the first bit to Taco, and he curled up next to me, sucking it like a stick of rock. I grinned at Paige, over his head.

'Tomorrow *we'll* get tents,' I said. 'I've never camped before. How about you and Bob? Do you have camping holidays?'

I felt her draw back—the way a snail does if you try and touch it. 'Can't be worse than this,' she said gruffly. Then she turned away and started eating her bread, without waiting for Muriel to toast it.

10

NEXT MORNING, THERE was chaos. The second batch of tents arrived—and the TV cameras came with them.

When the delivery lorry pulled in through the gates, there was a line of cars and vans behind it. They must have been expected, because Bernadette was there to brief the journalists and show them around.

But they didn't want to stay together, of course. Each of them wanted *the* picture of Lemon Dough— and *the* story of desperate, starving refugees. Before they'd been there half an hour, they were roaming all over the camp, chattering in a dozen different languages. Interviewing people and filming the mud and the makeshift shelters.

One group homed in on us. Justin and Bob had gone off to help put up the tents, and I was at the taps, filling our bucket, so there was no one there except Paige and Taco. And the cameraman wanted some film of Taco looking brave and pathetic.

So they set him up with my bike.

They'd dragged it out from underneath the polythene and got him to hold the handlebars. Which made him look very small, of course. And then someone had the bright idea of putting him up on the saddle.

When I came back with the water, he was halfway down the hill, shrieking with excitement as he headed for the bottom fence. And the broken spokes were *clack-clack-clacking* as they whirled round and scraped the front forks.

I went berserk. I dropped the bucket and ran after the bike, in a fury. 'What are you doing, Taco Bannister?' I yelled. 'You'll wreck that wheel! Get off—now!'

But he couldn't, of course. He couldn't do anything except hang on frantically, waiting for the crash when he hit the fence. It was sure to happen. Certain. There was no way—

Then at the last moment, out of nowhere, a man ran towards the bike and grabbed Taco, lifting him into the air. The bike careered on, straight into the fence, and the man put Taco down and then marched up the hill. He started shouting at the cameraman who'd put Taco up on the bike.

'What were you thinking of? He could have broken his neck.'

The cameraman shrugged. 'Hey, Salman, there's no harm done. And it's a brilliant shot. Look.'

He held out his camera, but the man he'd called Salman brushed it away. He was white hot with anger. 'These children aren't toys for you to play with. We're here to report, not to interfere. And what about the bike? Maybe you've damaged that.'

'It's only an old wreck,' the cameraman said. 'Look at it.'

Salman turned round and looked. I'd pushed the bike back up the hill, holding the front wheel off the ground to protect it. Maybe there was something about the way I was handling it that caught his attention because he came over and spoke to me.

'I'm sorry about my colleagues,' he said. 'They find it hard to look at disaster all the time and sometimes they do stupid things.'

'It's much harder for us,' I said angrily. 'They should try *living* here. They can go home whenever they like.'

'They're not your enemies,' Salman said. 'They're on your side. We all are.'

Huh! I thought. It must have shown in my face, because he leaned forward suddenly, as if he really wanted me to believe him.

'We have to report on this,' he said. 'So the rest of the world doesn't forget all about you. It's *important*.'

I wasn't convinced. He would say that, wouldn't he? He was a journalist, like all the others.

But Taco thought he was great. He'd just managed to struggle back up the hill and he came racing across and threw himself at Salman. 'That was brilliant!' he shouted. 'Can we do it again? Please?'

'I don't think your brother would be pleased,' Salman said. 'It's his bike, isn't it?' He glanced at it. 'And it's not a wreck at all. Just needs a few new spokes.'

'I'll fit those,' I said. 'When I can get some.'

'That's good.' Salman studied my face for a moment. Then he said, 'Look—camps like this are always tough. I've seen dozens of them, all over the world, and the people who come through best are the people who make things happen. So go out and find those spokes and fix up your bike. That's how to keep your self-respect. Do something *worthwhile*.'

He grinned down at me and patted the handlebars. Then he lifted his head and looked across the field. The new tents were going up quickly now.

'I need to see what's happening with those,' Salman said. 'I hope they give you one of them. Good luck.'

'Thanks,' I said. And I watched him march away across the field, with the rest of his team trailing after him.

Taco sidled up to me. 'I'm sorry,' he said in a small voice. 'Is your bike all right?'

I shook my head. 'You've broken two more spokes,' I said. But somehow I'd stopped being angry. I pushed the bike back to our little shelter and watched Paige shaking water off the polythene.

'Next time you want to get rid of a bucket, throw it somewhere else,' she said sharply. 'It's too cold for water games.'

They let us into one of the new tents just as it was getting dark. We were in between Bob and Paige on one side and Kara and her three grandchildren on the other. It was a relief to have somewhere dry at last.

But you can forget everything you know about camping holidays. OK, we did have a tent and a couple of camp beds (I was sharing with Taco, of course). And it was cold and wet. And the toilets were two fields away. Most camping holidays seem to be like that. But there's one big difference.

If you're on a camping holiday, you can always pack up and go home.

You've probably got a car, as well. All we had was the tent, and everything had to be crammed into it. That evening, we just shoved things in on top of each other and fell asleep in the middle of the mess, but we had to sort it out in the morning—and it was like doing a jigsaw puzzle.

I didn't think we had much stuff, but every space was full. Our bags just fitted under the beds, but we still had to find room for the bucket and the mugs and the washbowl that came with the tent. And the bike—

'That's staying outside,' Justin said.

'No!' I wasn't having that. 'It'll get wet. Or stolen.'

'Matt, it's broken,' Justin said. 'It's no use.'

'I don't care.' I held on to the bike and glared at him. 'It's coming inside.'

I thought I'd have to fight for it, but Justin suddenly gave a sigh—a bit like a balloon going down. 'Do what you like,' he said. 'I'm going to have a bit of a rest. I'm shattered.'

There was something unsettling about the way he said it. As if being tired was a relief. As if he couldn't wait to hide away under the covers. I didn't want to think about that, so I turned my back on him and dragged the bike inside. I padlocked it to the frame, opposite the little wood-burning stove.

Justin was right, of course. It was horribly in the way. But he edged round it without saying a word and lay down on his camp bed, with his eyes closed.

What were we supposed to do? Sit and stare at him?

116

'I'm going out,' I said loudly.

He didn't open his eyes. 'Take Taco with you,' he said. And he turned over, with his back to us.

Taco knew something was wrong. He looked at me with his mouth trembling—which meant I had to pretend everything was OK.

'Let's go and see if there's any more bread,' I said brightly. 'We can make our own toast now. Come on—I'll race you.'

That usually gets him going, but he was very slow that morning. So I took his hand and hauled him up to the top of our field. When we reached the gate, we could see there was something happening up at the sports centre. The crowd by the tap stands was buzzing with excitement.

Then Paige came running down the hill towards us, with an empty bucket in her hand. She must have gone up to fetch water, but she'd come back without it.

'What's up?' I shouted.

'Fetch your papers,' she muttered as she raced past. '*Quick!* Then get into the queue.'

'What queue?' I said.

She didn't stop. Just looked back, over her shoulder. 'Food vouchers. Hurry!'

I told Taco to stay where he was and then ran back into the tent, as fast as I could. Justin seemed to be asleep, so I didn't waste time on him. I pulled the big rucksack from under his bed and felt in the front pocket for our registration form—the paper that proved we had a right to be there.

I was just going to race off again when I had another thought and I grovelled under the other bed, for my backpack. The bundle of money Mum gave me was right at the bottom, where I'd hidden it when I snatched it away from Paige. I pulled off the rubber band and took a couple of twenty pound notes. Then I ran back to Taco.

'We've got to hurry,' I said.

He looked as if he was going to cry, so I grabbed his hand and dragged him up the hill. There was already a queue stretching out of the sports centre. I joined the end, as fast as I could, and patted Taco's arm, so he knew he'd done well.

Bob and Paige were half a dozen places ahead of me, almost at the door. When Bob saw us, he came down the queue and said, 'Where's Justin?'

'He's in bed,' I said. 'When I've got the vouchers I'll tell him—'

Bob shook his head. 'You can't afford to waste time. As soon as you've got the vouchers you need to head straight into town. Before the supermarkets sell out of the cheapest things.'

'I can't go on my own,' I said. 'How will I know what to buy?'

'Ask Muriel.' Bob nodded up the queue, to show me where she was. 'She walked into town yesterday and spotted all the best prices. Paige is going with her.'

'But Taco—'

'I'll look after him,' Bob said. 'There's some kids playing football down in the bottom field. Fancy a game, Taco?'

Lucky Taco! I wished I could play football instead of going shopping.

By the time I reached the front of the queue, Muriel and Paige were coming out with vouchers in their hands. Muriel waved hers in my face.

'*This* isn't going to buy much,' she said, sounding disgusted. 'And it's supposed to last us a *month*. We need to buy the big packets—economy size—and share them with each other. OK?'

Was that sensible? I didn't know. Paige saw me hesitating and gave me a sharp, impatient nudge.

'You're doing it. Right?' she said. 'Give him a bit of your shopping list, Muriel.'

Muriel pulled it out of her pocket. 'There are three supermarkets. You can go to the one by the church. That's where rice is cheapest—and one or two other things.' She tore off the bottom of the list and pressed it into my hand. 'Get as much as you can and then meet us in the square.'

She and Paige went off, without waiting for me, and I shuffled forward two more steps towards the door.

If only I'd had the bike! By the time I got our food vouchers, there were *dozens* of people walking up to the town. I went as fast as I could, jogging most of the way, and I overtook quite a few of them, but the supermarket was full by the time I got there.

And the vouchers hardly bought anything. I went round with a basket and picked up two big bags of cheap rice, two kilos of dried beans and a tube of tomato paste. Then I stood in the aisle for ten minutes, adding everything up over and over again, to see how much flour I could afford.

People kept pushing past me. It was easy to spot the ones from Lemon Dough, not just because they were scruffy, but because they were concentrating so hard. They didn't take any notice of me—but the people from the town were different. They muttered when they passed me and some of them shoved me out of the way.

A couple of old grannies stopped to take a look in my basket. They weren't sly about it. They just waddled up and peered in, frowning and clicking their tongues. Then one of them said something sharp to me, in French. When I shook my head—to show I didn't understand— she screwed up her mouth and spat on my shopping.

Right on to a bag of rice.

It was like being hit. I couldn't say anything. I just froze until they went away and then rubbed the spit off and dried my hand on my jeans. *It's nothing*, I told myself. *Just a couple of silly old women.* But I couldn't stop shaking. And when I went to the checkout, I kept my eyes down, so I wouldn't have to look at anyone.

The man at the till held out a couple of carrier bags. I loaded the shopping into them and then handed over my vouchers. He checked them, very carefully—and then held out his hand, as if he wanted some money as well.

'No,' I said. 'I've paid with the vouchers.' I pointed at them, to make him understand.

He shook his head and tapped the bags.

I did a silly mime, pretending to add up on my fingers and then pointing at the vouchers again, to show that the vouchers were Enough For All The Food In The Bags. The man replied by taking a couple of coins out of his till and waving them under my nose.

I didn't know what to do. When they gave me the vouchers, at Lemon Dough, they said all the shops in town would take them. Was that wrong? Didn't they work here?

And if they didn't work—could I get them back?

For one panicky moment, I thought I was going to land up with no food and no vouchers either.

Then a girl from the next queue tapped me on the shoulder.

'The bags,' she said. 'You have to pay for the bags.' She had a very foreign voice and it took me a moment to realize she was speaking English.

When I understood, I took out the only money I had—the twenty pound notes I'd pushed into my pocket. I held one of them out to the man at the till.

The man lurched back as if I'd insulted him, brushing the notes away with his hand. And some of the people behind me started to laugh, pointing at the notes and falling about at the joke.

Stupid English boy. Thinking anyone would want *his* money!

I went bright red and emptied my shopping out of the carriers. All I could do was carry the food away in my arms. That wasn't easy, because it was in fat, slippery polythene bags, but I hugged the bags to my chest and scuttled out of the shop.

Paige was walking round the square, looking in all the shop windows and Muriel was sitting under a tree, feeding Charlotte. They had lots of pasta and a little bit of oil and cheese. And a couple of courgettes Paige had got for nothing because they were going mouldy at one end. I didn't tell them what had happened in the shop.

We walked back to Lemon Dough together and took everything to Muriel's tent, to divide up the food. There were no scales to weigh it, or boxes to store our share. Muriel measured it out in mugs and tipped it into freezer bags for us.

'You'll have to come back for the oil,' she said. 'Bring one of your own mugs.'

As I set off back to our tent, I saw Taco racing past with a couple of dozen other kids. They seemed to be playing a weird game of football, without any rules, running between the rows of tents and sliding on the wet mud.

I stood and watched them for a moment. It was very noisy, because they were all yelling, and every time anyone kicked the ball it bounced off one of the tents and left muddy marks.

The mud didn't stay outside either. Some of the tents were open at both ends and one of the girls was kicking the ball right *through* them, to loud cheers from all the other players.

'Don't you *dare* do that to our tent,' I said to Taco as I went past.

He grinned at me and stuck his tongue out.

By the time I reached the tent, Justin had managed to get out of bed. He looked at the bags and said, 'Is that meant to last us a *month*?'

'You do it next time!' I said. 'Where can I put it all?'

He thought about it. 'How about one of the back-packs? We can hang it from the tent frame and keep the food off the ground.'

'We can use mine,' I said. I dumped the bags on his bed and went to empty it out. There wasn't much. Just the tool roll—that went straight back under the bed—and a few spare clothes that I tucked in on top, under the blanket.

And the roll of money.

I felt sick when I pulled that out. There were hundreds of pounds there—and it was just rubbish. *Rubbish!* I threw the whole lot out of the tent, as far away as I could. Then I dropped the food bags into the backpack, fastened the top and used a sock to tie it to the tent frame.

Justin took charge of the cooking that evening—dragging himself to the stove as if it was a massive effort. All we had was some pasta with a minute amount of tomato paste, but it took him ages to make. He counted every piece of pasta.

'We have to make sure it lasts,' he said.

I heard Taco scuffling about outside the tent. I didn't bother to look out and see what he was doing. I just shouted. 'Come on! Food!'

He ran in and knelt down to get at his bag under the bed. I saw him pushing something into his precious shoebox. What on earth had he found? There was nothing in Lemon Dough except mud and more mud.

He tied up the bag and came across to the stove to take a look in the pan. When he saw what Justin was stirring, he pulled a face.

'Is that *all?* What's for pudding?'

'No pudding,' Justin said. He dropped a spoonful into a plastic bowl. 'This is it.'

Taco scowled. 'But I'm *hungry.*'

Justin flared up at him. 'Of course you're hungry!' he shouted. 'What do you expect me to do about it? All we've got is what we're given. We're so useless that *other people have to feed us.*'

Taco was too shocked to speak. He stared at Justin, with two big tears trickling down his face.

When Justin saw them, he crumpled. 'I'm sorry, Taco. It's not your fault. I didn't mean to shout. I'm just *so tired.*' He sat down and pulled Taco on to his lap and we ate our pasta together, without talking.

It didn't take long.

We swilled the bowls out with clean water and then drank the water to try and fill ourselves up a bit more. Before we'd finished, Justin was looking longingly into the tent, though it wasn't even *beginning* to get dark.

'Go to bed,' I said. 'I'll look after Taco.'

'Is that all right?' Justin said. 'I just need a bit of a rest, that's all. I'll be OK soon.' He crawled into the tent and Taco came and snuggled up to me.

'Is it always going to be like this?' he said, in a small, nervous voice. 'Will things never be good again?'

I looked down at his narrow little face and thought, *You don't even remember the really good times.* 'It's getting better already,' I said. 'We've got food now, and a tent. And soon we'll have a proper home again.'

'With Mum?' Taco said.

'Of course. And she'll cook fantastic meals, the way she always does.'

'With tacos?'

The way he said it, I almost burst into tears myself. 'There'll be *lots* of tacos,' I said. 'More than you can eat. Every day, if you want.'

Taco gave a kind of sigh and leaned his head against my chest, looking up at the stars. 'You know,' he said after a moment, 'I don't *exactly* remember what they're like. But I love them, don't I?'

'You *adore* them,' I said. 'They're like giant crisps— only a million times better.'

Taco gave a long sigh. 'Oh yes. I remember.' But I could tell he didn't.

When I woke up next morning, I lay there for a bit, waiting to see if anything would happen. Then I sat up and looked across the tent.

'Justin?' I said.

'No point in getting up yet,' he mumbled. He turned away and pulled the blanket over his head.

I looked at my watch and thought, *But it's almost ten o'clock.* Taco was sitting on the ground, playing with something underneath our bed. When I looked down at him, he scooped it up and stuffed it into his shoebox, smacking the lid on quickly, so I wouldn't see.

'Is there anything for breakfast?' he said hopefully.

'No chance,' I said. I swung my legs off the bed and tried to think of something to distract him. 'Shall we go and see Muriel?'

'Yay!' Taco said. He pushed his shoebox right under the bed and stood up. 'Can we go now?'

We had to wear all our clothes in bed, just to keep warm, so we didn't need to waste time getting dressed. But maybe we could wash a bit.

'Let's see if there's any water,' I said.

There was an inch or so at the bottom of the bucket. I took it outside and we splashed our faces and dried them on our sleeves. Paige was sitting cross-legged on the ground outside the tent next door, staring at nothing.

'We're going to see Muriel,' Taco said.

Paige unwound her long legs and stood up. 'Maybe I'll come too,' she said. 'Doesn't look as if anything else is going to happen.'

We slithered up into the next field together. Muriel's tent was right by the gate, and she was delighted to see us. She came running out of her tent, waving a big iron saucepan.

'Look what I've found!' She was very excited. 'I took Charlotte for a walk up the road and there it was, lying in the corner of a field. Someone must have *thrown it away*. Isn't that strange?' She waved it again and Paige ducked just before it hit her face.

'That's never going to fit on your stove,' I said.

'Don't need the stove,' Muriel said. 'I'll make a fire. When I was in the peace camp—' We didn't find out what had happened there, because Charlotte started yelling inside the tent. Muriel sighed and looked at Taco. 'Fancy playing with her? Then I can look for stones for my fireplace.'

Taco didn't need asking twice. He ducked inside the tent and Charlotte stopped crying and gurgled at him.

Paige was looking doubtfully at the saucepan. 'What are you going to cook in there? You'll never get enough food to fill it.'

'Yes I will,' Muriel said enthusiastically. 'I'm going to make soup. And anyone can share it, if they bring something to go in the pot.'

Paige raised an eyebrow. 'Like?'

'Oh—I don't know.' Muriel shrugged. 'There must be something in those woods. That's where I was heading when I found the saucepan.' She pointed along the road, away from the town. 'I bet there are mushrooms in there. And nettles. And dandelion leaves. Why don't you go and look? Wait a minute.' She dived into the tent and came out with a plastic carrier bag. 'Make sure you bring it back.'

It all sounded weird to me. Dandelion leaves? Nettles? 'Can you really eat those things?' I said.

Paige looked at me as if I was a fool. 'Don't be such a townie.' She marched away up the hill, as though she didn't care whether I followed or not.

I nearly didn't. But then—what else was there to do?

By the time I caught her, she was up by the gate, talking to the Bernadette woman who'd registered us. And she looked like a different person. Not just because speaking French did funny things to the shape of her mouth, but because she was *laughing*. And Bernadette was laughing too. But they didn't tell me the joke.

'They lock up at sunset,' Paige said over her shoulder. 'As long as we're back by then, we can do what we like.' Then she was through the gate and out, heading away from the town, as if she didn't care whether I followed or not.

The road ran down to the bottom of the valley, between huge fields with no fences in between. Just two big stretches of open land, covered in sunflowers on one side and something tall and green on the other. There were no hedgerows where we might have found nuts and berries. Only the verges at the side of the road—and someone had obviously been along there already, picking anything that might be good to eat. All we found was one dusty dandelion, trampled flat at the side of the road. It was covered in grey dust, but Paige picked the leaves anyway and put them in Muriel's bag.

We reached the bottom and the road started sloping up again, towards the little wood Muriel had pointed out.

'There might be rabbits in there,' I said.

'Yeah?' Paige said sarcastically. 'And how are you going to catch those? With your bare hands?'

'We can cut off your hair,' I said solemnly. Making it up as I went along. 'I'll plait it into a long cord and tie a loop in one end.'

Paige stared at me, but I managed not to laugh.

'Then we can hang it from a low branch,' I said. 'And when the rabbit comes by—'

Suddenly she got it and she started laughing—shaking so hard that she had to stop and lean against a road sign.

I pretended not to notice. 'When we've caught the first rabbit,' I said, 'we can use its sinews as a bowstring. And sharpen its bones to make arrowheads. Then we can shoot a pigeon, and that'll give us feathers for the arrows and—and—'

I couldn't keep it up any longer. We were just at the edge of the wood by then and I turned aside, into the trees, laughing till I thought I would choke.

'You're daft,' Paige said. 'Totally daft.' It was the nicest thing she'd said to me. She bent her head and peered between the trees, into the darkness of the wood. 'It doesn't look like the sort of wood that has picnic tables and nature trails. But there might be some mushrooms. Come on.' She started along a little path that led away from the road and into the trees.

'Stop,' I said. 'You'll get lost.'

She gave me her *you are a worm* look and kept on walking.

'*Paige!*'

'Don't be silly,' she said, over her shoulder. 'This path is going downhill, right? So if we want to get back, all we have to do is go *up*. You don't need A levels to work that out.'

I didn't think it could be that simple, but she obviously wasn't going to stop. So I started along the path behind her, jogging to catch up.

'Lots of nettles,' she said cheerfully. 'You'd better pick some of those.' She bent down and held the bag open. 'Come on. What's stopping you?'

'But I'll get stung,' I said.

She nodded gravely. 'That's right. Your hands will swell up like balloons. You won't be able to get your fleece off. And Taco will have to feed you and change your trousers.'

I pulled a face at her and dragged my sleeves down over my hands. 'No he won't! Look—I've foiled your evil plan!'

I picked half a bagful of nettles and then we wandered on down the path, stopping two or three times when there was something worth picking. I'd just bent down to grab some more dandelions when Paige slapped her hand on my shoulder.

'Sssh!' she said fiercely. And she lifted her face and sniffed at the air.

I thought she was still kidding around, so I copied her. I lifted my face and sniffed too—only much harder, as if I was in a cartoon and my nose was ten feet long.

And I smelt wood smoke. And roasting meat.

Sssh, Paige's mouth said again. Only this time she didn't let out any sound. She left the path and began creeping off down the slope, peering into the trees ahead of us. At first I thought it was another joke. Then I saw how tense she was.

Maybe we ought to go back, I wanted to say.

But the smell of cooking drew me down the slope after her. It was months since I'd tasted any kind of meat.

We heard voices before we saw anyone. They were talking so quietly I couldn't hear much more than a vague rumbling sound and we were almost at the clearing before I realized I could understand the words.

They were speaking English.

There were three of them—teenagers with torn clothes and dirty, unshaven faces. They were sitting round a very small fire in the middle of the clearing. Beyond them were a couple of small green tents, camouflaged with branches. One of them was holding something on a long stick, turning it slowly over the fire.

Was it a rabbit? A pigeon? I couldn't make any sense of the shape until Paige put her mouth against my ear and breathed 'Chicken'. It was small and scrawny, and one side was starting to burn.

The boys were arguing about whether it was ready to eat. One of them snatched at a leg—and then whipped his fingers away and shoved them in his mouth.

'Roasted finger!' said one of the others—and he licked his lips.

It didn't feel like a joke. They were all looking too hard at the chicken. They wanted it too much, and their mouths were like hungry caves in the firelight. Dark holes, waiting to be filled.

What if they saw us?

I looked at Paige and she frowned and shook her head. *Stay out of sight.* I wished we could creep away—but suppose they heard?

The boy with the burnt fingers wrapped his jacket round them and pulled at the chicken again. This time half of it came away in his hand—and the rest dropped into the fire. The others swore at him and snatched the meat up, yelping as the flames licked at their arms. They started tearing at the joints with their teeth, sucking the juice from their fingers.

Paige crouched down, leaning forward slightly, as if she was waiting for something. I caught hold of her sleeve, to stop her doing anything stupid, but she pushed me away impatiently and went on staring into the clearing.

The boys spent a long time eating, turning the bones over and over in their hands and hunting for a few more scraps of meat. But finally they gave up—and they threw the chicken bones over their shoulders, into the bushes.

That was what Paige had been waiting for.

As they started raking their fire together, throwing on more bits of wood, she went down on her hands and knees and crawled forward carefully. Then she reached out very slowly—like playing Jenga—and tried to pick up the bones without rustling any of the bushes or shaking the branches.

She almost did it. But the last thigh bone was just too far away. As she reached for it, her weight shifted forward and there was the crack of a dry branch breaking.

The boys whirled round. 'Who's that?' one of them shouted. 'You spying on us?'

We didn't waste time answering that. We ducked back into the trees and ran.

11

WE COULDN'T CHOOSE which way to go. All we could do was try and stay together. Paige had the longest legs and I found myself following her, slipping on wet branches and trying to rip away the brambles that tangled round my legs.

The boys were stronger and faster than we were—but we were *smaller*. We zigzagged between the trees, slipping through gaps that were too narrow for them, and running straight under branches they had to duck. We could hear them crashing after us, but the noise grew further and further away and finally Paige came to a stream and stopped to listen.

'I think they've given up,' she said.

I doubled over, trying to catch my breath. 'Did we really—need to run?'

Paige nodded slowly. 'I think they're hiding out,' she said. 'They're too old to be in Lemon Dough. If the police find them, they'll send them back to England.'

I thought about that. 'But they wouldn't—do anything, would they? If they caught us?'

Paige shrugged. 'We can test it out if you like. Shall we go back that way?'

'Ha ha.' I looked round slowly. 'Any idea where we are?'

'It's easy,' Paige said. 'I told you. If we go uphill, we'll get back to the road.'

'Are you sure?' I glanced up, to see where the sun was, but the whole sky was covered in cloud and I couldn't decide which way we were facing.

'Of course I'm sure,' Paige said scornfully. She pointed off to the right. 'We need to go *that* way and the track will be at the top. Come on.'

We started battling our way up the slope, watching for the break in the trees where the track went through. But we couldn't see it. And when we reached the top we found—

No track.

'Oh,' Paige said. 'I was sure—'

'At least we won't starve to death,' I said lightly. 'We've got all those juicy chicken bones. And *nettles*. Yum.' I peered into the trees ahead, where the ground sloped down again. 'Maybe that path doesn't *stay* on top of the hill. Maybe it went down into the next valley. I think there's a bit of a clearing down there. Shall we go and look?'

'Don't see what else we can do,' Paige said gloomily. 'Unless you want to go back?'

I thought of those boys and their angry, violent shouts. 'No,' I said. 'I don't think that's a good idea. We'd better go on.'

We slithered down the slope, hanging on to branches to stop ourselves going too fast. I was right. There was a clearing at the bottom—but it wasn't our track.

We found ourselves looking down into an untidy yard, with a small, dilapidated house on one side. There was an overgrown vegetable patch opposite the house and a half-ruined barn facing us across the yard. Washing hung on a line between the house and the barn and three scrawny chickens were scratching around under a plum tree.

'Shall we ask the way back?' I said.

Paige looked at the chickens. Then she looked at the chicken bones, still clutched in her hand. 'Might be tactful to tidy up first,' she said lightly. She dropped the bones into Muriel's bag, muttering 'Ouch!' as she pushed them under the nettles. Then we slithered down the rest of the slope and came out of the trees and into the yard.

I was planning to knock on the door of the house, but there was no need. As soon as we came out into the open, a little terrier shot out of the barn and threw itself at us, barking manically. Two seconds later, a woman opened the door of the house.

I'd expected someone old and decrepit. But the woman wasn't old at all. She was very young—hardly grown-up—with a tired face and long, tangled hair. A little boy peered out at us from behind her legs. He looked around Taco's age, but much shyer and more nervous.

When the woman saw us, she frowned and started shouting. I would have run away, but Paige grabbed my arm and pulled me forward, calling out to the woman in French.

It took a few moments for the shouting to stop, but Paige wasn't put off by that. She just went on talking and smiling, as if there was no problem, and gradually things quietened down. The woman came out into the yard and caught hold of the dog, to stop him jumping up at us. I think Paige was asking for directions, because the woman began nodding and pointing through the trees. But I couldn't understand a word, so I started looking round instead.

And suddenly I saw what was in the barn.

The rickety door was standing open and beyond it, in the shadows, was a heap of half a dozen old bikes, leaning against a wooden pillar. They didn't look as if anyone ever rode them.

But they all had wheels. With spokes. And some of them looked as if they might be the same size as mine.

I couldn't take my eyes off those bikes. For a second, I even thought of telling Paige about them. Getting her to ask if I could have a few spokes—just half a dozen or so—because they obviously weren't being used.

But even though the woman had calmed down a lot, she didn't look as though she would hand out spare parts for nothing. And if we didn't go soon, she might start wondering why the dog was so interested in our carrier bag. So I just stared into the barn and kept my mouth shut.

The woman pointed again and said something else and Paige turned back to me. 'We're not far from the road,' she said, 'but it's quite a distance back to the camp. We'd better get going.'

She said something else in French and then headed across the yard. The woman stood watching us go, with the dog beside her, and the little boy gazing at us from the doorway, with his mouth wide open.

Paige was marching off down the stony track, without waiting for me. When I caught up with her, she was very quiet, striding along with her head down and her hands in her pockets.

'What's the matter?' I said.

'That poor woman!' she muttered. 'Do you know she used to have *twenty* chickens? And they've all been stolen now, except those three in the yard. *Les anglais,* she kept saying. C'*est des anglais qui m'ont volé les poules.*'

'What?' I said.

Paige shoved me impatiently. 'Why don't you learn some French? She said it was the English who stole her chickens.'

I thought of the boys in the wood. 'Did you tell her about them?'

'You mean—tell her she was right? Let her know the English *are* a load of dirty chicken rustlers? Of course I didn't. But I wish—' She shook her head and marched on down the track and out on to the road.

I've never seen anyone as happy as Muriel when we turned up with those chicken bones. She'd built a little fire in one corner of her field—out of sight of the soldiers—and the big saucepan was simmering away, balanced on a circle of stones. The soup already smelt pretty good and there were half a dozen people waiting to taste it.

Paige pulled the bones out of her pocket and Muriel grabbed them. 'Just what I need,' she said. 'Now this soup is *really* going to work.' She dropped the bones into the pot and went on stirring, rocking Charlotte's carrier with one foot.

We had to wait for it. It was another couple of hours before she decided the soup was ready. By then, there were a dozen people standing round the fire, holding out cups and bowls and plastic boxes. Muriel spooned the soup out carefully, giving each of us a fair share. Then she grinned over our shoulders—at all the other people who were watching.

'Sorry—that's it,' she said. 'But I might make some more tomorrow. Bring something to go in it. Oh—and some wood for the fire.'

'Hope that saucepan stretches,' Bob muttered under his breath.

There was a kind of magic about Muriel's soup. There wasn't much for each person, but it was very tasty—and *it wasn't stale bread*. The fire was warm and comforting too. We sat around it for a long time after the soup was finished, talking and staring into the embers. Charlotte fell asleep on Muriel's lap and Taco snuggled in between me and Justin, humming happily to himself.

I kept thinking about the house Paige and I had found in the woods. About those bikes, going to waste in the barn. It was wicked the way that woman was letting them rot away. And I only needed a few miserable spokes. If I sneaked into the barn and took them, she'd never even notice.

But I couldn't sneak in, because that little dog would start barking. And she'd catch me before I was halfway across the yard.

I had to work out a way to distract the dog . . .

12

I DREAMED ABOUT those spokes. In my dream, I was in the barn with my own bike and I was working on my front wheel, replacing the broken spokes. I could see the light from the barn doorway glinting on the handlebars and feel my fingers working the spoke ends into the holes in the wheel hub.

It was so clear, so real, that I must have been making the movements in my sleep, nudging against Taco. He started pushing back and I woke up suddenly, just as I was about to topple off the bed. And once I was awake, it was impossible to get back to sleep. My mind kept going back to those bikes, trying to work out a way to sneak into the barn without being given away by that wretched little dog.

In old stories, people always drug the dog, with sleeping tablets hidden in a piece of steak. But that was wilder than fantasy. No one I knew ever had any meat to spare. If they had it, they ate it. And there wasn't any meat at all in Lemon Dough.

I had to think of something else.

Taco was still asleep, but I'd disturbed him and he was wriggling around, trying to get comfortable. Then he bashed his feet against the bike at the end of the bed and he woke up too.

'Stupid bike!' he mumbled. 'It's no use. Why don't you throw it away?'

'Sssh!' I whispered into his ear. 'It just needs some new spokes, that's all.'

Taco squirmed round, sticking his elbow in my stomach. It was a very thin, bony elbow. 'But there's nowhere to buy them. And you threw all your money away.'

(Maybe I should have asked him how he knew that. But it didn't seem important just then. Not compared with the bike.)

'I know where I could *get* some spokes,' I said. 'If only I had someone to help me.'

My voice was too loud and Justin reared up suddenly, waking with a shout. 'Shut it, you two! I've *got* to get some sleep or I won't be able to cope!'

That disturbed Kara next door and she called out softly. 'Please be quiet, or you'll wake the children.'

Then people started hushing *her*, of course—*Ssssh! Ssssh! Ssssh!* Until it sounded as if a wind was blowing through the camp.

In the middle of it all, Taco put his wet little mouth against my ear and whispered, 'I'll help you. If you like.'

I bent my head down, to whisper back. 'With the spokes?'

He nodded sleepily. 'I'll help you get them, so you can mend your bike. When are we going to do it?'

I glanced down the tent, to make sure Justin wasn't watching us. Then I whispered very, very softly, 'We could do it tomorrow. If you like.'

'All right,' Taco mumbled. 'Is it a secret?'

'It's a big secret. You mustn't tell anyone. Promise?'

'Cross my heart and hope to die,' Taco said solemnly. Then he curled up against my side and went back to sleep.

Next morning, Justin actually got up. But only just. He dragged himself up the hill to get some water—and then he went back to bed again.

'We'll eat this afternoon,' he said dully, as he kicked off his shoes. 'You can play till then.'

'Only one meal?' Taco said wistfully.

'Sorry,' Justin said—as if he was too exhausted to care. 'Can't manage any more. We have to last out till the next food vouchers.' He lay back and closed his eyes.

'We'll leave you in peace,' I said quickly. 'Be back around one o'clock.' I slipped on my backpack—with the tool roll hidden inside. Then I grabbed Taco's hand and headed for the gates.

As we walked away down the road, I told him about the bikes in the ruined barn. Laying it on really thick about how they were being wasted there and how it wouldn't make any difference *at all* if I took just a few of them. Then—when I saw he was happy about all that—I told him what I wanted him to do.

'It's not a *dangerous* dog,' I said. 'I wouldn't be taking you if it was dangerous, would I? It's just friendly— and very small. All I need you to do is distract it a bit. So when the woman comes out she thinks the dog's barking at you, not me. You can do that, can't you? You're good with dogs.'

Taco looked worried. 'But what will I *say*? I haven't learnt enough French yet.'

'That's *good*,' I said. 'The woman will concentrate on making you understand—and she won't have any time to notice me.'

I kept walking down the road, pulling him along with me. He grumbled when we got to the hill, but I didn't let him stop.

'You promised,' I said. 'And it's not far now.'

We slogged up the road and over the hill and then turned down towards the chicken woman's house. Taco frowned when he saw the track.

'It's not even a proper road. How can anyone live down here?'

'That's what it's like in the country,' I said.

'But suppose there's a man with a gun?' Taco stopped suddenly, staring down the path.

'No one's going to shoot you.' I tried not to sound impatient. 'We're going to hide in the bushes until the yard's empty. Then I'll dash into the barn and you wander about as if you're lost. And talk to the dog.'

'But it's a *French* dog.'

'Don't be silly,' I said. 'Dogs just talk Dog. It's the same everywhere. Now keep quiet. We're almost there.'

We crept down towards the house, walking on the grass at the side of the track. When we came in sight of the yard, I stopped with my finger on my lips. The woman was outside, taking in some washing, and the little dog was sniffing around near the house. I thought it might smell us, but the wind was blowing the other way.

The woman unpegged the last few garments and dropped them into the clothes basket. Then she picked up the basket and went into the house. The

148

dog lifted its head and looked around for a moment, then it padded after her.

I gave them a minute, to get right inside, and then I nodded to Taco. 'OK, here we go. Don't worry. When she sees that you're lost, she'll show you this track and you can go round the bend and wait for me there. And if anything goes wrong, I'll come and rescue you. Deal?'

'Deal,' Taco said solemnly.

I patted his arm and then shot up the track, into the yard and straight through the doorway of the barn. I was just inside when the dog began to bark and I crouched down and crossed my fingers hard. If Taco didn't come, I was finished.

But he did come. Looking through the open doorway, I saw him wandering into the yard, with the strange, vague expression he has when he's scared and he's pretending not to be. The dog had just charged out of the house, heading for the barn, but it stopped for a second when it saw him.

'Hello,' Taco said brightly. And then, '*Comment allez-vous?*'

The dog hesitated. Then it started barking again and the woman appeared in the doorway. Her little boy was beside her, chewing a piece of bread and jam.

Taco's eyes homed in on the jam. He didn't say anything. Just stared at it with his eyes looking very big in his thin, pale face.

The woman rattled off a whole stream of French. She sounded very angry and I thought Taco might run away. But he didn't. He looked up at her and said his bit of French again. *'Bonjour. Comment allez-vous?'* Then his eyes went straight back to the jam. And the little boy who was eating it.

The woman hesitated for a moment. Then she pointed first at the bread and then at Taco. And she put her head on one side, as if she was asking a question.

Taco got it straight away. 'Yes!' he said. With a huge grin on his face. *'Please!'*

The woman gave a little nod and held out her hand. Taco looked at it for a second. Then he put his hand into hers and the three of them went into the house, with the dog following them.

I hadn't expected that. Taco knew all about not going off with strangers, but he didn't even look round to see if I was watching. Just took hold of her hand and let her lead him inside—like Hansel and Gretel going into the gingerbread house.

I knew I should go and get him out again. Straight away. But that would have ruined everything. I was there to get the spokes, and there would never be a better chance than this. So I pushed Taco to the back of my mind—just for a few minutes—and concentrated on the bikes instead.

There were six of them altogether, leaning in a heap against the post. Filthy old wrecks, with warped front wheels and rusty frames. One of them was a child's bike and one was a battered old racer, but the others all looked the right size.

How lucky was that?

I could have taken all the spokes from one bike. That would have been quicker, but it would have ruined that bike. If I took a couple of spokes from each of them, it might not make much difference. I opened my tool roll, slipped out the tyre levers and started on the first bike.

It's fiddly getting spokes out. First you have to remove the tyre, the inner tube and the strip that goes round the rim. I had to do all that *four times* and then unscrew the spokes and hook them out of the hub. I took two spokes from each bike—eight altogether— and wrapped them up in the tool roll. Then I put back all the tyres and made sure I left the bikes exactly where they'd been when I found them.

As I leaned them against the pillar, I thought, *They're not too bad really. It wouldn't take much work to fix most of them.*

But it was only a quick flutter in my mind. Nothing serious.

When I had everything packed up, I peeped round the barn door to see if Taco was outside again. There was no sign of him. I took a deep breath and scooted out of the yard and back up the track. But when I reached the bend, he wasn't there either. So he must still be inside the house.

I stashed the tool roll—with the spokes—in the middle of a thick bush. Then I crept back to the edge of the yard and waited for him to appear.

But he didn't come.

After ten minutes, I started getting anxious.

After twenty minutes, I really thought there must be something wrong.

After half an hour, I knew I had to go in and fetch him.

I started creeping towards the house, to see if I could wave at him through the window. But I didn't stand a chance of getting there. Before I was anywhere near, the little dog started barking his head off inside the house. So I changed my plan. I marched straight up to the front door and knocked hard. Then I opened it and put my head inside.

'Taco?' I said.

The little dog flung itself at my legs and the woman was close behind. She wrenched the door wide open, took one look at me and started yelling.

'It's no use,' I said. 'I can't understand a word. I've just come for my brother.' I pointed past her, into the house. 'My *brother*,' I said. 'Taco.'

'Taco?' His name worked like magic. As soon as she heard it, her face cleared and she stepped back to let me inside.

Taco was kneeling on the rug in front of the fire, playing with the boy I'd seen before. They were building a long spiral ramp out of cardboard and sticky tape. And next to them, lying at the end of the rug was another dog. A huge black one, lying quietly with its head on its paws.

Suppose that *one had run out at Taco. He would have been so scared . . .*

I didn't let myself imagine it.

'Taco!' I said quickly. 'What are you *doing*?'

He turned round and beamed at me. There was jam all over his face. 'Look!' he said excitedly. 'Pierre and I made this. Isn't it fantastic?' He picked up a little toy car and dropped it on to the top of the ramp. It zoomed round the spiral, all the way to the bottom. And when it reached the ground it hit a plastic brick and somersaulted across the floor. Taco and the little boy burst into screams of hysterical laughter.

The woman laughed too. She pointed at the boy and said, 'Pierre.' And then something else. I didn't understand the words, but I could tell what she meant by the way she looked at me. It was a question.

'Matthew,' I said.

She smiled and tapped herself on the chest. 'Steff.'

Taco grinned up at her. 'Can I come back tomorrow?'

'Don't be silly,' I muttered. 'Come on, Taco. We're not here to make friends. *You know we've got to go.*'

Taco picked up the car and sent it down the ramp again.

'*Taco,*' I said.

'OK, OK.' He pulled a face and stood up. 'Bye, Pierre,' he said. '*Au revoir.*'

Pierre waved his hand and said something I didn't understand. Taco didn't understand either, but as we went out I could hear him muttering it under his breath.

'*À demain, à demain, à demain . . .*'

'Stop that,' I said. 'What are you doing?'

'I'm remembering.' He frowned, the way he did when he was concentrating. 'So I can ask Paige when we get back.'

It was really irritating, but I knew it was no use telling him to stop. And anyway he deserved to be let alone. He'd done just what I wanted—only better. We went round the bend in the track and I picked up my tools and the spokes. And I let Taco chant his rubbishy words all the way back to the camp.

I could hardly wait to get my bike out and fit the spokes. But it's no good rushing at a complicated job. That's what Grandpa used to say. When we got back to Lemon Dough, Justin was cooking some rice and after we'd eaten that—as slowly as we could—he sent me up to the taps to fill the water bucket.

After that, it was too late to begin work. I knew the light wouldn't last until I'd finished the job. So I waited until the next morning before I began.

By then, I'd had time to think about where I was going to do it. I didn't want lots of people disturbing me and asking questions, so I went behind the tent and trampled the weeds that were growing there, next to the fence. I turned the bike upside down and found some heavy stones to wedge it in place. Then I tied the wheels together, spread my tool roll out on the ground and started work.

As I was taking out the first broken spoke, I heard a voice on the other side of the tent.

'Pai-aige?' It was Taco.

Paige's voice muttered something I couldn't catch, and then I heard Taco again. I didn't understand what he said—but I recognized the sound. It was the French words he'd been repeating on the way back yesterday. The words Pierre had said to him.

Adderman. Sevah? That's what it sounded like.

Paige laughed. 'Adder madder, sadder, vadder,' she said.

'*No,*' Taco sounded cross. 'It's *French*. I want to know what it means.' And he said it again, a bit slower.

'Actually, you've got quite a good accent,' Paige said. 'It means *See you tomorrow. OK?* Who said that?'

Taco hesitated. Then he muttered, 'I'm not allowed to say. It's a big secret.'

Oh great! Now Paige really would be interested. I wondered whether to go round and say something to put her off, but before I could think of anything that might work there was another voice. This time it was just behind me.

'That looks professional.'

I looked over my shoulder and there was Bob. He was standing with his hands in his pockets, looking at the tools, and the bike, and the spokes laid out in a neat row on the ground.

'Just mending my bike,' I said.

Bob nodded. 'I can see you know what you're doing.'

'You've got to be organized,' I said. I started wriggling the broken end out of the wheel hub. 'If you don't keep things straight, you'll likely do more harm than good.' Grandpa used to say that too.

Bob laughed—as if it sounded funny coming from me. But he didn't go away. 'Let's see you then,' he said. And he stood there, waiting for me to carry on.

I didn't really like the way he stared—it was very sharp and concentrated—but I wasn't going to let him

156

put me off. I picked up the spoke wrench and started unscrewing the next one.

Bob stood there while I cleared all the wreckage out of the way and put in the first replacement spoke. I was picking up the second when he squatted down beside me. He lifted up a couple of spokes and turned them over in his hands.

'Where did you get these?' he said.

I didn't look up. 'Found them, didn't I?'

Bob ran his finger along them. 'They're not new.'

'Took them off an old wrecked bike,' I said. As if it was no big deal.

The moment the words were out, I knew they were stupid. Bob was sure to ask me lots of awkward questions now.

But he didn't. He just stayed there watching me. After a while, I almost forgot about him. It's tricky, replacing a lot of spokes at once. If you're not careful, you can put too much stress on the old ones and pull the wheel out of true. By the time I started tightening everything up, I'd almost forgotten about Bob. I was concentrating on the sound and the feel of the spokes as I twanged them, making sure the tension was the same all the way round.

Bob didn't say a word all the time I was doing that. He didn't speak until I untied the front wheel and spun it round against my hand—to check it was still a circle. Then he said, 'Suppose there were—other bikes that needed mending. Reckon you could find spares to fix those?'

His voice was very careful, as if he meant a bit more than the words were saying. I spun the wheel again, thinking of the rusty old bikes in the barn. 'Maybe,' I said. 'Some.' I sounded careful too.

Bob looked down at the tool roll. 'You know,' he said thoughtfully, 'what you want in a place like this is something that makes you special. Something you can *trade*. Like that bloke in the top field who's found a way of charging phones. He's building up a nice little business. Everyone wants their phone charged up—and he lets them pay him in food if they haven't got any money. You could do something like that.'

'But there are lots of phones,' I said. 'Has anyone else got a bike?'

Bob grinned. 'You'd be surprised. I reckon we'd do OK with a bike repair business.'

I wiped my hands on a bit of rag. 'We?' I said.

Bob laughed and tweaked my ear. 'There's more to business than getting your hands oily. You have to let people know what's available—without making too much fuss. And you have to work out how much to charge them. Could you do that?'

'I . . . um . . . '

'And make sure you get paid?'

'Maybe not.' I looked up at him. 'But I still don't see where the bikes would come from.'

'Why don't you leave that to me?' Bob said. He looked me straight in the eye. 'If you do the work, I'll bring in the business. What do you say?'

There was a moment that felt like balancing on the edge of something. *What am I getting myself into?* Then I nodded. 'OK. If you find the bikes, I'll do my best to mend them.'

Bob grinned and tapped his fingers on my shoulder. 'Good lad. You won't be sorry.'

Then he went off and I cleaned my tools and put them away—wondering what kind of repairs I'd be able to manage. I had a couple of spare inner tubes and a bit of brake cable. And there were lots of patches in the puncture repair kit. But that was about it.

Unless I went back and raided Steff's barn again.

I was still thinking about it when Justin trailed round the end of the tent. He was frowning. 'Where's Taco?' he said.

I shook my head. 'No idea. I heard him talking to Paige, but that was a while ago. Don't know where he went after—'

And then it hit me. What he and Paige had been saying. He'd jabbered something French at her—the words Pierre had said yesterday—and she'd told him what it meant. *See you tomorrow. OK?*

See you tomorrow . . .

He couldn't have gone back to Steff's, could he? Not on his *own?*

13

I TOOK A long breath. No point in worrying Justin. Yet. 'Maybe I'll go and ask Paige,' I said.

Justin nodded. 'Tell him I'm cooking soon. Don't want to waste the food.'

I rolled up my tools and stashed them in the tent. When I'd padlocked the bike in its place, I went up the field to the phone charger queue. I guessed Paige would be there.

'Hey,' I said, 'where's Taco?'

She raised an eyebrow at me. 'Seemed to think he had somewhere to go. Don't know where it was, but he must have been there yesterday. With someone French.'

My heart gave a thud. 'You let him go?'

'It's not my job to look after him,' Paige said quickly.

He's only six! I wanted to shout. But being angry would only waste time. I looked over her shoulder, hoping to catch a glimpse of Taco walking up the road, but there was no sign of him. So maybe—

'The soldiers wouldn't let him out of the camp, would they?' I said. 'Not on his own.'

Paige shrugged. 'They're not paid to be nannies. Anyway, he wouldn't need to go through the gate, would he?'

'What do you mean?'

'There's a hole in the fence. Down in the corner of the bottom field.' Paige looked scornfully at me. 'I thought *everyone* knew that.'

'But how could Taco—?'

'They were playing football down there yesterday. He must have seen it. I bet he went out that way.'

I started running down the hill, towards the corner where the hole had to be. But as I passed our tent I realized I had a faster way of travelling now. I ducked inside—ignoring Justin—and unlocked my bike. Then I hurried back up to the gate.

When I was almost there, Paige came running across to meet me. 'I'd better come with you,' she said crossly. 'He must have gone to see someone French— and *you* won't be able to talk to them.'

'Don't bother!' I panted, still walking. I was still annoyed with her. 'I'll do it on my own.'

'That's silly.' Paige was impatient now. 'You won't be able to *talk* if there's any trouble. They must be French people. I'm coming.'

'I've got my bike,' I muttered.

'No problem,' Paige said.

There wasn't time to argue. I ignored her and headed out through the gate and she kept pace with me. She ran up the slope, almost as fast as I could pedal, so when I reached the turn into the woods I stopped for a second, to let her catch up.

She gave me an odd look. 'You think he's gone there?' she said. 'But how did he know—?' She stopped short. 'OK, let's not waste time. You get on—and I'll be right behind you.'

I free-wheeled down the track, bumping over stones and swerving to stay out of the ruts. When I reached the bottom, I looked back and there was Paige strolling after me, with her head bent, as if she was thinking.

In front of me, the chickens were having a dust bath in the yard. When they saw me, they scuttled about fussily, squawking and fluttering. And—of course—before I'd taken more than a couple of steps, the little dog raced out and started barking.

Steff came out and stood in the doorway, shading her eyes against the sun. When she saw me, her mouth tightened and she said something sharp. I looked back for Paige, so she could tell me what it meant, but she was only halfway down the slope.

'Taco?' I said hopefully, pointing to the house.

Steff gave me a long, cold stare. And then she shouted. 'César!'

The big dog came shooting out of the house. His body was like a battering ram and he put his head down and jumped straight at me. I collapsed in a heap on the ground, and my legs tangled up with the bike. *No!* I thought. *Not more broken spokes! Please—*

I couldn't look. The dog had its front paws on my chest and Steff was standing over me in a fury, clenching her fists and bellowing.

'Paige,' I shouted. '*Paige!*'

Paige legged it down the slope. She was shouting too, and waving her hands around, and as soon as she was near enough she launched into a fast, fierce burst of French. For a couple of seconds she and Steff were both talking at once.

Then Paige went very quiet.

'What's going on?' I said.

Paige looked down at me. 'What did you do to her bikes?' she said coldly.

Taco was standing in the doorway now, with Pierre beside him. They both looked terrified—but Taco looked much worse because he was scruffy as well. And dirty. And thin.

'I didn't do anything,' I muttered.

'Don't waste time,' Paige said. 'You must have come back here—or how would Taco have found this place?

And suddenly your bike's all mended. So what did you take?'

I looked at her. How could I argue? Unless she did my talking for me, I'd never get the dog off my chest. 'All right,' I said. 'I'll show her what I did—if she calls this thing off me.'

Paige seemed to be talking for ever, but finally Steff stopped glaring and took a step back. All of a sudden, she looked very tired. 'César,' she said again, in a different voice.

The dog backed off and stood glaring at me, with a growl hovering at the back of its throat. I unwound my legs from the bike, taking a quick look at the spokes (OK, thank goodness!) and grinned at Taco as I stood up. I didn't want him worrying.

'We'll have to go into the barn,' I said. 'So I can show her.'

Paige passed that on and Steff gave a sharp little nod. I pushed my bike across to the barn and leaned it against the front wall, tapping the spokes and showing eight fingers. Then I led the way inside.

When I saw the bikes again, I suddenly stopped feeling stupid and embarrassed and I started feeling *angry*. It made me sick to see them heaped up together like a load of scrap metal.

'All I did was take a few spokes,' I said to Paige. 'Why should she care? She's not doing anything with them. Just letting them rot away. They're good, solid bikes and they ought to be out on the road. But look at them!'

'They're her bikes,' Paige said. 'Not yours.'

'Well why doesn't she look after them? It wouldn't take much to fix them up. But no, she'd rather see them fall to bits and be *wasted*. You know what? I'm *glad* I took those spokes! At least they're being useful!'

I didn't even know I was shouting, until Taco slid in beside me. He clung on to my arm, giving it quick little pats, the way he did when I was angry with him. Suddenly I heard my own voice and I felt stupid again.

Steff looked at Paige and raised one eyebrow. *What was all that about?*

I don't know what Paige told her. It wasn't much— just a couple of sentences—but somehow it changed everything. Steff stared at me for a second and then she turned and walked out of the barn, beckoning us to follow her.

'Seems like you did something good after all,' Paige muttered. 'Want to see where this takes us? Or shall we head for the hills?'

I would have run, but Taco was pulling me towards the house. And after all, what could happen? If anyone started talking about the police, I'd just go into the barn and put the spokes back.

But Steff hadn't *looked* as if she was going to call the police.

I went across the yard, with Taco babbling away at me. He'd obviously been there for quite a while, because he and Pierre had built another huge track for the toy cars. This time it was a network of tunnels, made of cardboard rolls and sheets of newspaper. It went all round the room, climbing over the chairs and twisting through the legs of the table.

Steff put out glasses on the table. One for each of us. She filled them with something red, out of a jug, and then she took out a rubbery brown cake and peeled off four or five slices on to a plate. When that was done, she waved her hand at the table. Paige sat down and took a gulp of the red liquid.

'What is it?' I said. 'Is it wine?'

'Of course not,' Paige said scornfully. 'It's grenadine. Have some. And the cake's a bit like gingerbread.'

I sat down cautiously and sipped. The grenadine was very sweet. And the cake was delicious. I couldn't remember when I'd last had cake. I ate it very slowly, tasting each crumb.

Steff waited until I'd finished. Then she sat down opposite me and fired off another sharp question. I caught the words *Lemon Dough* and I knew what she was asking.

'They all hate the camp,' Paige said under her breath. 'They're angry because we get food for nothing and they have to work for it—even though things are very hard here. And they think we go round stealing and smashing things up.'

'I don't smash things up,' I said fiercely. 'I *mend* them. I'd mend those bikes of hers, if she let me.'

Paige blinked at me for a second. 'That's good,' she said slowly. And she leaned across the table and started explaining.

Steff watched my face carefully, as if she was making up her mind about something. Then she stood up and beckoned, to show that we were going out to the barn again. We trailed back across the yard, with Taco hanging on to my hand.

When we got there, Steff pulled the oldest, most rundown bike off the top of the heap and looked at Paige. What she said was very short, but I could tell it wasn't a question.

'She wants you to fix that one,' Paige said.

I didn't need to think about it. 'Not a hope,' I said. 'Look at the state of the frame. And the forks. I can't do anything to make those safe. But I could use some of the parts to mend a couple of the other bikes—as long as she buys new tyres.'

Paige fed that back and Steff gave a quick little nod. I hadn't realized it was a test, but it looked as though I'd passed. And the next question was serious.

'Do you want paying?' Paige translated.

168

I hadn't even thought about money. For a second I thought, *That's brilliant!* Then I thought a bit more—and shook my head. 'Tell her I'll do the first bike for nothing. I owe her for those spokes.'

When Steff heard that, she finally relaxed and gave me a proper grin.

I grinned back. 'Tell her I'll come tomorrow,' I said. 'And bring my tools.'

Steff nodded and smiled again. Then she went back inside and brought out the rest of the rubbery cake. I thought we were each going to get another slice, but she wrapped the paper round it and pressed the whole thing into Paige's hand.

That was awesome.

It took a couple of minutes to convince Taco that we had to leave. I persuaded him in the end, by saying he could ride all the way back to Lemon Dough. But as I pushed the bike down the track, he kept twisting round and shouting over his shoulder to Pierre.

'*Au 'voir! Au 'voir, Pierre! A demain!*'

His mouth made silly shapes when he talked French, as if he was pretending to be someone else. Paige made it worse, by teaching him new words, all the way home. She made him repeat them over and over again, until they sounded French enough.

It would have driven me mad if I'd listened. But I blocked it out by thinking of the most *un*French words I could. I didn't say them out loud, but I ran them over and over in my head. *Fish and chips, Big Ben, London, cricket, Man U, dandelion and burdock, the Queen* . . .

Reminders of real life.

When we got back to our tent, there was a pan of cold cooked pasta on the stove. Nothing else. Just pasta. And Justin was back in bed.

'Is that for us?' I said.

Justin muttered, 'Yes,' and sat up, very slowly, as if he was going to come and serve it out for us.

'Don't bother,' I said. 'We can look after ourselves.'

I put half of it into a mug for Taco and gave myself the saucepan. We sat on the ground outside the tent and ate it slowly, without talking. When we'd almost finished, Bob came drifting down from his tent.

'Present from Paige,' he said. He gave me a lump of Steff's cake and looked over my shoulder, into the tent. 'How's your dad?'

'He's not my dad,' I said. 'And he's in bed. Keeps saying he's tired.' I hesitated. 'You don't—think he's ill, do you?'

'No-o,' Bob said carefully. 'He's not ill. But he's very—' He broke off without finishing. 'Just tell him I was asking after him, OK? You two all right?'

'We're fine,' I said. 'Aren't we, Taco?'

Taco nodded, with his mouth full of pasta, and Bob walked back up to his own tent. I went into ours and stood by Justin's bed. 'Bob came to see how you were,' I said.

Justin heaved himself up slowly and swung his legs round until he was sitting on the edge of the bed. But he didn't stand up. 'I can't seem to get going,' he said. He looked dreadful. He hadn't shaved for almost a week now and his face was very pale under the stubble—except for the red, cobbled lumps on his cheek.

'How *is* that?' I said, looking at it.

'Getting better.' He put a hand up and touched it lightly. 'Soon be back to normal.' For a second I thought he was going to stand up. Then he said, 'Anything need doing?' I shook my head and he lay down again.

I watched him for a moment before I went outside again. Taco and I each ate a slice of Steff's cake—and then we ate the last two slices as well. I meant to save a piece for Justin, but once we started we just couldn't stop.

When it was all finished, Taco stood up. 'Going to see Paige,' he said. 'I need to learn some more French.' He went up to their tent and I swilled out the pasta saucepan and drank the water.

Then I wondered what to do.

I didn't want to listen to Paige and Taco spouting French, but I didn't fancy sitting on my own either—especially not with Justin lying around in the tent. So I put the saucepan away and went to see Muriel.

She was busy making some kind of flat, floury pancakes, patting them out into circles and cooking them on a sheet of old metal she'd picked up somewhere. When she saw me, she tore a pancake in half and held out a piece.

'Fancy some of this?'

I hesitated. 'I haven't got anything—'

'For heaven's sake!' she said sharply. 'I'm not trading. You can have it for nothing. Here.'

'Sorry.' I took the pancake and sat down. 'Thank you. That's really nice of you.'

'I like feeding people,' Muriel said. She bit a piece off her pancake and chewed it energetically. Then she picked Charlotte out of the carrier and gave her some. 'What d'you think?' she said.

I tried mine. It was tough and rubbery, but there was something—'Hey! You've got *salt*!'

Muriel grinned. 'That was pretty much all I had when I left England. A bag of salt. So I brought it with me. Makes a difference, doesn't it?'

'This is like real food.' I took another bite. 'Wish I could cook properly.'

'These are easy,' Muriel said. 'I'll teach you. Hang on—let's see your hands first.'

They were filthy from working on the bike. Clicking her tongue disapprovingly, she pulled a bit of rag out of her pocket and dipped it into her water bucket. Then she scrubbed away at my hands until they were clean.

I remembered how Mum used to fuss about washing before meals. I hadn't even thought about doing that since we left home.

Muriel spread the rag out by the stove to dry and inspected my hands again. 'That's better,' she said. 'Now I'll show you. And next time we get food vouchers you can buy some flour and make your own. They're great. Go with everything.' She tipped some flour into a bowl and opened the bag of salt. 'This is how I do it.'

I watched her hands as she kneaded the dough and patted it into shape. It was like watching Grandpa working in his shed. She made the same sort of strong, confident movements.

She broke off a piece of dough and gave it to me and I tried to copy what she was doing. It was harder than it looked, but after a while I started to get the hang of it.

'It's good making food with other people,' Muriel said. 'Cooking and eating together. This place would be a lot better if we did more of it.' And she leaned over and tweaked my dough, just slightly, to make it a perfect circle.

14

I WAS PLANNING to spend the whole of the next day at Steff's working on the first bike. I woke up very early and lay in bed inventing stories to tell Justin, so I didn't have to explain what I was really doing.

But I needn't have bothered. When I said, 'I'm going out for a while,' he didn't ask any questions. He lifted his head a couple of inches off the bed and muttered. 'Take Taco with you.' And that was it.

It would have been nice to go on my own. In the camp, there were always people around. You were never away from their noise and smell and the constant moving about. But I couldn't leave Taco by himself. Not with Justin like that.

'OK,' I said. 'We'll be back in time to eat.'

I unlocked my bike and shook Taco until he woke up. 'We're going to Steff's,' I said. 'Come along.'

He stretched like a little cat, blinking at me as he pushed the covers back. 'No breakfast?'

'No breakfast,' I said. 'But you can wash your face if you like.'

He took the lid off the bucket and stared at the water. It looked very cold.

'Don't think I'm really dirty,' he said.

I let him ride on the back of the bike. I would never have done that at home—Mum was very strict about things like that—but things were different now. He hung on round my waist and he was so light that I reckoned I could pedal all the way up the hill and along the track without having to make him get off.

As we zoomed down the road, Paige was watching us from inside the fence. Taco waved at her, so hard he nearly fell off—just as a car was overtaking us.

'Hold on properly!' I shouted. 'Or I'll make you walk there.'

He hates it when I'm angry with him. He buried his face in my back and I thought he might be crying, but I couldn't help it. I'd shouted because I was scared. It felt as though there was no one else to look after Taco. Only me.

'Sorry,' I said. 'Just hang on properly. OK?' Taco nodded and I put my head down and pedalled hard. I wanted to get to Steff's as soon as I could.

I hadn't thought about what day it was. After all, what difference did it make? In Lemon Dough, we went to sleep when it was dark and woke up when it was light and nothing much happened in between. I'd lost track of the days of the week, and it didn't occur to me that they might matter to Steff. Not until we turned up in her yard and she and the little dog came out to see us.

When she saw Taco, she frowned.

Then Pierre appeared in the doorway, with a piece of bread in his hand. He was wearing long trousers and a shirt, and his hair was neatly combed. He looked quite different.

I'd forgotten all about school.

France was a country for holidays, wasn't it? I'd never thought about people there going to work and doing ordinary things. But Pierre was dressed for school, and so there wouldn't be anyone for Taco to play with.

Steff didn't want to share their breakfast with us either. When Pierre waved his bread at Taco, she tapped his wrist quickly, to make him stop. Looking embarrassed, as if she wished they had enough for us too.

I pointed at the barn—to show we were going there—and whispered in Taco's ear. 'Pierre's going to school, so you'll have to stay with me. And I don't think they've got any spare food. Tell Steff we've had our breakfast already.'

Taco frowned. 'I don't know how to say that.'

'Think of a way. She won't want you to come if she thinks she has to feed you all the time.'

Taco gave the bread a longing look. Then he grinned at Steff and went into an amazing pantomime. First he pointed to the bread and shook his head cheerfully. Then he pointed into his mouth with one hand and back towards the camp—more or less—with the other, nodding enthusiastically. It took a while for Steff to work out what he meant, but he kept on miming until she laughed and ruffled his hair.

Then she said something in French. Taco repeated it and she shook her head and said it again. Over and over, until he copied her. I couldn't see any point in hanging around to listen to that, so I went off into the barn.

It was very quiet in there—so quiet I could hear the sound of my blood going round—and the light came softly through the door, catching the specks of dust floating over my head. Nothing else was moving. And there was nobody there but me. For a moment I stood quite still, staring at it all.

It didn't look as though anyone had swept the floor for a hundred years. It was covered in dust and dry leaves and bits of ancient birds' nests. I found a ragged old broom and cleared a space in the middle of the floor, so I had somewhere clean to work. Then I unrolled my tools and laid them out.

I'd already decided which bike to start on. It was a chunky little road bike. It needed a new set of brake pads and a few spokes—to replace the ones I'd taken. And when I tested out the gears I found that one of the cables was broken. That meant stripping off all the handlebar tape and putting in a new one. I'd seen Grandpa do that—once—and it was quite complicated. I was still working out *exactly* what he'd done when Steff's old red truck started up. A couple of minutes later, Taco appeared in the doorway.

'Pierre's gone to school,' he said in an odd voice.

'I told you he would,' I said.

'But what about me?' Taco wandered into the barn and stared at the bikes. 'Why aren't I going too?'

'You wouldn't understand what the teacher says. And there probably isn't room for all the kids from Lemon Dough anyway.'

'But if I don't go to school I won't learn anything,' Taco said. 'I'll be *stupid*.'

'No you won't,' I said.

'*Everyone* goes to school.'

'You can learn things outside school,' I said. 'Why don't you do that? Help me with the bike.'

Taco hesitated. Then he nodded solemnly and edged into the barn. I cleared him a place to sit and started showing him what I was doing.

When I'm working on something complicated, I like to concentrate and forget everything else. But Taco wouldn't let me forget. He kept pointing at things and asking questions.

'Why is there tape round the handlebars?'

'To keep the cables tidy. I have to take it off before I can put in new ones—and I'm going to try and save the old tape. So don't jog me.'

Taco froze—I swear he was holding his breath—and I started winding the tape round the corner. I was about halfway when I realized there was someone standing behind us, watching. I forgot I hadn't heard the pickup coming back and I thought it was Steff, so I went on winding to show her how careful I was. I didn't look round until I'd finished.

And it wasn't Steff at all. It was Bob.

'You're making a nice job of that,' he said.

I couldn't believe it was him. 'How did you find us?'

'Paige told me about this place. So I thought I'd come and take a look.' Bob turned round and studied the chickens and the untidy yard. 'It's a real find. We can do a lot here.'

I didn't know what he meant. 'But it's not ours. It belongs to Steff.'

'Of course,' Bob said. 'Of course it's hers. But she's not coping, is she? Look at that vegetable patch.'

He was right there. The vegetable patch was chaos. It was choked with thistles and nettles and there was bindweed crawling up the raspberry canes, pulling them right down to the ground.

'She could do with a bit of help, couldn't she?' Bob said.

I thought he meant me. 'I'm doing the bikes,' I muttered. 'Can't manage anything else.'

'Of course not!' Bob grinned. 'But Justin could give her a hand. You ought to get him down here.'

'Justin?' *But he won't even get out of bed.*

Bob put his head on one side and looked at me for a moment. 'Think about it,' he said. 'He needs a bit of work to take his mind off things.' He gave me a slow smile and then walked away, crossing the yard and disappearing into the trees.

When Bob thought of something, it always seemed to happen. Next morning, Taco and I were just crawling out of bed when Paige wandered across from the tent next door. 'You off to Steff's?' she said. As if she was just chatting. 'OK if I come along too?'

Justin lifted his head. 'Steff?' he said. As if he'd heard her name somewhere before.

'She lives over the hill,' Paige said. Sounding bored. 'You *must* know her. Taco's really friendly with her little boy.'

I knew what she was up to. She was pressing the Bad Dad button. *Are you letting your children go off with strangers?*

Justin sat up and looked at Taco. 'Have you been going out of the camp?' he said. 'On your own?'

Taco gave him an angelic smile. 'Matthew took me. He's mending Steff's bike. She's *nice*. She lets me and Pierre build car tracks and she gives me bread and jam.'

Paige raised her eyebrows at Justin and he sighed and stood up. 'Suppose I'd better come and see what you're getting up to. Where is this place?'

'You're not going like *that*, are you?' I said, before I could stop myself. He hadn't washed for days and his chin was covered in stubble. With that and the swelling on his cheek, he looked wild and scary.

He groaned and picked up the bucket. 'Better go and fetch some water,' he muttered. And he struck off up the hill.

I glared at Paige. 'OK. What's all this about?'

'Just did what Bob told me to,' she said. 'Don't you think it's a good idea?'

'What?' said Taco. 'What are you talking about?'

'Justin's coming to Steff's,' Paige said lightly. 'And if he sees her vegetable patch, *maybe* he'll feel like sorting it out. Then we can all have lovely fresh vegetables.'

'She doesn't have to share them,' I said grumpily. I wasn't sure I wanted Justin hanging around at Steff's. 'It's *her* garden.'

'Of course she'll share them,' Paige said. 'She's not a lousy rotten scadger.' Her eyes glittered as she grinned at me and I felt my throat grow dry.

Steff must have been taking Pierre to school, because the pickup had gone and the dogs weren't there.

Justin walked into the yard and looked around vaguely until he spotted the vegetable patch. When he saw it, he went across and stared for a moment or two. 'Bob didn't say it was *that* bad,' he muttered.

I stood by the barn door, pretending to talk to Paige and Taco. But really I was watching Justin. Almost absent-mindedly, he crouched down and started disentangling the bindweed from the raspberries. Unwinding the shoots slowly and carefully so he wouldn't snap the raspberry canes. After a moment or two, he looked about and found a stone so that he could get out the roots.

Paige and Taco wandered off together. Taco was chattering about building a bridge for his car track and Paige was nodding and picking up loose branches and old bits of wood. I left them to get on with it and went into the barn.

But I'd only just laid out my tools when Steff drove back into the yard. The pickup stopped, the door slammed and I heard Paige shouting something cheerful.

Steff started to answer—and then she broke off short. There was an angry shout and the sound of feet running across the yard.

I ran to the barn door and saw Steff standing over Justin, shrieking at him in French. He obviously didn't have a clue what she was talking about.

'It's all right!' Paige shouted. 'Justin, why don't you show her—?' Then she switched to French and shouted at Steff instead.

But Steff didn't stop. It sounded as if she *couldn't* stop. As if all that rage had been bottled up inside her and now it had to come out. I couldn't understand a word of what she was yelling, but I knew what it meant all right.

She'd never seen Justin before in her life, and she didn't care who he was. I don't think she'd even noticed he was trying to help her. All she could see was a dirty, unshaven man from Lemon Dough and that was enough to set her off. She looked like those two old women in the supermarket. Angry and scornful.

Then César leapt out of the back of the pickup and raced towards Justin, snarling horribly. Paige threw herself across the yard and seized Steff by the shoulder, screeching into her ear. For a moment everything was exploding at once. Paige and Steff were shouting, the dog was barking and Taco was sobbing with terror.

Then Steff said, 'César!' in the voice that meant, *Stop!* And the dog froze, with its teeth a centimetre away from Justin's leg.

'Justin—show her the weeds,' Paige said. 'Quickly! She thinks you're stealing her vegetables.'

Justin reached out with his foot and stirred the heap of bindweed beside him. Then he looked up at Steff. 'I'm not a thief,' he said. 'But I do know how to grow vegetables. I could sort this out for you.'

Steff frowned for a moment, as Paige translated. Then she looked at Justin for a long time, studying his face very carefully.

She and Justin made a bargain. If he got the vegetable patch organized, we could have a third of everything it grew. It didn't sound much to me, but Steff and Justin were very happy about it. He dug over half the patch before we left and Steff gave him a couple of muddy old roots to mark the deal.

184

Justin whistled all the way back to Lemon Dough and as we went past Muriel's tent he stuck his head in and waved the roots at her.

'Fancy a turnip?'

There was a delighted yelp from inside the tent. 'Where did you get *that*?' Muriel came bombing out with a grin on her face. 'I'll put it in my bean stew.'

Justin dropped one of the roots into her hand. 'We'll be over in half an hour.' He looked at me. 'And after that—we could trade some rice for a phone call. Do you fancy talking to your mum?'

'Yay!' said Taco. He was so excited he danced all the way back to our tent, running backwards and forwards to try and make Justin hurry. It was the best moment since we'd left home.

When we got back to the tent, Justin put some water on to heat and took out his razor.

'Better make myself respectable,' he said solemnly. 'Can't talk to Ali with seven-day shadow on my chin.'

'But shaving takes *ages*,' Taco said. 'I want to talk to Mum *now*.'

Justin shook his head. 'After we've eaten. Then we can tell her you've had a good meal. She'll like that.'

'Now!' Taco said. 'Now, now, now—'

Justin splashed some water over his face. 'We'll be ready faster if someone fetches the rice. It's in my rucksack.'

'Me!' Taco shouted.

He blundered into the tent and reached for the rucksack. It was hanging from the frame and he didn't bother to take it down. Just undid the zip enough to slip his hand in. He pushed it down inside, feeling for the bag of rice—

—and then he screamed, a long, shrill scream that echoed all the way across the camp. He snatched his hand out of the rucksack, lifting it high in the air.

And there was a rat hanging from his thumb. Holding on by its teeth.

15

THE RAT WAS only there for a second. Then it dropped to the floor and flashed across the tent and away outside. And Taco stopped screaming and stood there, with his face dead white, staring at the blood running on to his jeans.

Justin dropped his razor and raced in, with soap all over his face. Bob and Paige were right behind him and Kara ran up from the other side, with her grandchildren following her.

By the time they arrived, Taco was sobbing hysterically. Justin picked him up and carried him outside and Kara caught hold of his arm.

'Let me look,' she said.

She pulled back Taco's sleeve. The rat had bitten into the fleshy part of his hand, between the thumb and the first finger, and blood was pouring out of it.

There was so much blood we couldn't see the wound itself, to know how big it was.

'Doctor ought to look at that,' Kara said. 'Take him up to the sports centre. There might be someone there.'

'Take Paige with you,' Bob said. He gave her a little push.

Justin started up the hill, with Taco in his arms, and as Paige caught up with him he looked back and shouted to me. 'Put the stove out, Matt.'

Kara put an arm round my shoulders. 'Bit of a shock?' she said.

I nodded. 'I've never seen a rat before.'

'It won't be the last time,' she said. 'This is rat heaven, with all the food lying around in these tents.'

Bob pulled a face. 'Let's make sure there aren't any more.'

He marched into the tent and gave the rucksack a heavy thump. Nothing moved. But when he untied the rucksack and lifted it down, rice started pouring out of a hole in the side.

'It's gnawed its way in,' Bob said. 'And bitten through one of your rice bags.'

'Don't waste the rice!' Kara called frantically. 'Catch it!'

'But the rat's been on it,' I said.

'For heaven's sake!' Kara pushed her way into the tent. 'You're going to boil it, aren't you? You can't waste all that food. And if you leave it lying around, you'll have *dozens* of rats flooding in.'

Bob and I started grovelling around, running our hands over the groundsheet and picking up every grain of rice we could find. Kara went back to her tent and found a carrier bag to put it in.

'People don't do this in the normal world,' I muttered. 'They'd just sweep it up and throw it away.'

'Depends what you mean by the normal world,' Kara said tartly. 'There's always people desperate for rice.'

We went on feeling around until there was nothing left to find. By that time Justin and Taco were back. And Justin was so angry he was shaking.

'There's no one up in the sports centre except a couple of aid workers. And all they could do was say, *Demain, demain.*'

'Tomorrow,' Paige said wearily. 'The doctor's coming tomorrow. But Taco might not even get to see him then. I talked to the soldiers and they said there's always a really long queue.'

Taco was curled up in Justin's arms, with his head lolling. He wasn't crying now, but he looked tired and scared.

'Poor little kid!' Kara said indignantly. 'Someone ought to do something.'

I didn't see what anyone *could* do, but Bob looked at Taco for a moment and said, 'Hang on a minute.' And he disappeared up the field.

'What *can* anyone do?' Justin said wearily. 'We'll just have to wait till tomorrow. But I ought to clean up Taco's hand now. Have a proper look at the bite.'

'No,' Taco said. In a very small voice. 'Leave it alone.' He curled his hand against his body, with the other one cupped round it.

'We ought to put something on it,' Justin said. 'Even if it's only salt water.'

Taco started whimpering and I thought he was going to burst into tears again. But before he could start, Bob came hurrying down the field with a tall thin woman carrying a bag.

'This is Amy,' he said cheerfully. 'She'll sort you out, Taco. She's a nurse.' He looked sideways at Justin and dropped his voice. 'She's got antiseptic and thread for stitching. But—she can't afford to do it for nothing.'

Amy had narrow, calculating eyes. She was staring at the open rucksack inside our tent. There were two bags of rice on top of it. One was Kara's carrier bag, with the rice we'd picked off the floor. The other one hadn't been opened at all.

Justin saw her looking. 'Will you do it for a bowl of rice?' he said. 'We're just going to cook some.'

'Dry rice,' Amy said. Folding her lips neatly around the words. 'I'll do it for a bowl of *dry* rice.'

190

That was three times as much as a bowl of cooked rice. It was a whole day's food for the three of us and I knew we hadn't got that much to spare. But how could Justin say no? He sighed and picked up Kara's carrier bag.

'No,' Amy said sharply. 'I'll have it from the other one. Where the rat hasn't been.' Justin hesitated—and she turned away, very slightly. Just so we knew she'd be off if she didn't get what she wanted.

That was all it took. Justin sighed and picked up the other bag of rice.

When he opened it, Amy produced a plastic bowl out of her nurse's bag. It was bigger than our bowls, and she held it out until Justin had filled it with dry rice, right to the top. Then she snapped the lid on and dropped it back into her bag.

It was getting dark by then. You don't really notice that in a house, where you can switch on the lights. But it makes a big difference when you're living in a tent. Amy glanced up at the sky and then she took a torch out of her bag. She pushed it at me.

'Shine this on his hand,' she said. 'And mind you hold it steady. I don't want to stick my needle in the wrong place.' She laughed at her own joke, with a flash of sharp little teeth. Then she picked up Taco's hand and studied it carefully and he looked away from her, chewing his bottom lip.

191

'OK,' Amy said brightly. 'Here we go!' She tipped some antiseptic on to a piece of gauze and gripped Taco firmly round the wrist. Ignoring his squeaks, she started cleaning up the wounds with brisk, firm strokes.

Justin stood behind Taco, stroking his shoulders and muttering soothing noises. It seemed to go on for ever, but somehow Taco managed to keep still while the bite was cleaned and stitched and dressed. He didn't start crying until Amy let go of his hand.

She wasn't interested in that. Giving his head a quick little pat, she dropped everything into her bag and snapped it shut. Then she went away up the hill, taking our rice with her.

'She's got three teenage boys to feed,' Bob said. As if that was an excuse.

Kara sniffed. 'Don't like to think what she's teaching them.' She looked at Taco. 'Don't cry now. You've been a really brave boy. Let me see if I can find a reward for you.'

She ducked into her tent and came out with a tiny notebook, no bigger than the palm of her hand.

'Have this,' she said. 'You can use it for collecting French words.'

Taco took the notebook in one hand and stared at it, wiping his eyes with the other. I could see he didn't know what to do with it.

'Shall I put it in your shoebox?' I said.

He hesitated. 'You won't look inside?'

'Of course not,' I said. 'Here.' I took the notebook out of his hand and he buried his face in Justin's shoulder again.

I didn't mean to look in the shoebox. I pulled it out from under our bed and raised the lid, just a little bit, to slip the notebook inside. But I couldn't, because the box was too full. I glanced back, to make sure Taco wasn't watching, and then lifted the lid right off.

And there was Mum's face, staring up at me out of the shadows. An old, battered photo that Taco must have picked up somewhere. Two little plastic astronauts were lying on top of it and a tiny cuddly stegosaurus with a purple body and orange spikes. There was a lot of paper or something underneath the photo, but I didn't want to poke about, so I just rearranged the astronauts and the dinosaur to make enough space for the notebook. Then I put the lid on and slid the box back under the bed.

When I went back outside. Kara was looking at the bag of dirty rice.

'That needs sorting out,' she said. 'Would you like me to cook some of it for you?'

I think Justin was going to say yes, but before he could answer Taco lifted his head. 'We're going to Muriel's,' he said. 'And then we're going to trade some rice and phone Mum.'

Bob raised his eyebrows. 'You're going to trade some *more* rice?'

As soon as he said it, I knew we couldn't spare any more. Not now Amy had taken so much of it. I saw Justin looking at Bob and I knew what he was thinking. *Will Bob let us use the phone for nothing? Just this once.* But Bob didn't meet his eyes.

Justin sighed. 'We'll have to leave the phone call for a couple of days,' he said. 'Sorry, Taco. We can't spare any more food this month.'

Next morning, Taco seemed absolutely fine. He managed to dress himself, in spite of his bandages. He was just doing up his trainers when he heard the sound of a ball being kicked around outside.

'I'm going to play!' he shouted. 'OK, Dad?' And he charged out of the tent without waiting for an answer. We heard him shouting for the ball, calling 'Me! Me!' as the game swirled round our tent and away down the hill.

Justin lifted his head off the bed and groaned. 'Those kids have got too much energy. They need *school*.'

'They're having fun,' I said. 'They can catch up with school when we get home.'

'You think they can wait?' Justin said. 'It could be *years*.'

194

I stared at him. 'But I thought—' We'd only come to France for a few months, hadn't we? Just until things got better—and people were bored with ScadgePost.

But suppose they didn't get better? Suddenly I had a picture of the time ahead of us, winding on and on into the distance. Like a long, grey tunnel, with no end in sight.

'We're not *living* here,' I said stubbornly. 'We've just got to get by till it's safe to go home again.'

Justin swung his legs off the camp bed and stood up. He was too tall for the tent and he had to crick his neck to stop his head scraping on the roof. Suddenly I wondered what would happen if we stayed for a year. Or five years. Or ten. Would his neck grow a permanent crick, till he couldn't straighten it any more?

He was still droning on about school. 'Taco needs to practise his reading. And learn to write better. And what about you? How will you cope with exams if you miss out on school?' He picked up the water bucket and headed out of the tent. 'I'll ask around in the water queue. See if there are any classes starting up.'

It would never work. OK, maybe someone could set up a school for little kids like Taco. They could always practise writing by scratching letters in the mud. But how could you have a *proper* school without books? And computers? And science equipment?

I'd learn more mending Steff's bikes than I would sitting in a field listening to someone pretending to be a teacher.

I pulled my tool roll from under the bed and put on my fleece. That was all it took to get ready. I was just about to go and find Justin, to tell him I was off, when Bob came scratching on the outside of the tent.

'Justin's not here,' I said. 'He's gone for water.'

'I didn't come to see Justin. It's you I want.' Bob stepped inside the tent. 'Remember that business we talked about setting up? Well, I think I've found your first customer.'

'What would I have to do?' I said cautiously.

Bob shrugged. 'He's got an old bike that needs fixing. If you can get it on the road, he could go off and look for work. And maybe he'll have some more bikes for you later on.'

There was something odd about that. 'You mean— he's French?'

Bob grinned. 'No, he's English, like us. So you ought to help him out.'

'He brought a bike he can't ride?'

Bob gave me a small, narrow-eyed smile. 'Maybe he didn't *come with* the bike. Maybe he—found it here. Lying around and going to waste. But we don't need to worry about that, do we?'

Do we?

You know that moment on a seesaw when your feet touch the ground and you can stop it moving if you want? All you have to do is stand up and hold the end steady. Or you can push with your feet and go shooting up in the air again. That's what it felt like, with Bob waiting for me to answer.

I pushed. 'And he'd pay me?'

Bob nodded. 'I told you, it'll be real money. I'll take care of all that. Why don't you come and take a look at the bike?'

'OK,' I said. 'Where is it?'

Bob led the way down the hill, right to the bottom of the field. There was a boy waiting there, hanging on to a battered old bike. I'd have guessed he was eighteen or nineteen, but that was too old for Lemon Dough. He was tall and skinny, with wild curly hair and a blue knitted hat.

'Hi, Scally,' Bob said. 'This is Matt.'

Scally looked me up and down. 'He's only a kid. You telling me he can mend bikes?' There was something familiar about his voice, but I couldn't work out where I'd heard it before.

'Trust me,' Bob said. He put a hand on my shoulder. 'Matt's the best there is. Why don't you let him take a look?'

Scally gave me another doubtful stare and then pushed the bike at me.

As soon as I saw it, I stopped worrying about where it had come from. He'd probably found it in a skip. It was filthy dirty and covered in rust and the brake pads were non-existent.

But none of that was a problem. I had some spare brake pads and cleaning up is easy. The real disaster was the front wheel. It was buckled so badly it wouldn't even turn when I tried to spin it. I didn't think Scally would be up for buying a brand new wheel, even if I could find one.

I was just going to tell him to take his bike away when I thought, *I know where there's a wheel going spare . . .*

The ruined bike in Steff's barn had one wheel that was totally useless. But the other one was fine, except for a few broken spokes. And I was pretty sure it was the same size as this one. So if I used the spokes from Scally's bike . . .

I ran my hands over the frame, as if I was examining it. But really I was making up my mind. By the time I lifted my head, I'd decided what to do.

'Yes, I can fix it,' I said. 'If you've got the money.'

Scally didn't ask any questions. He just put his hand in his pocket and pulled out a half a dozen French notes. Exactly the way Bob promised. Real money.

He wasn't about to hand it over, though. 'I can pay you, right? But you don't get anything till you've done the work.'

I wasn't going to let him trick me like that. 'Think I'm stupid? How do I know you'll pay me if I do it first?'

It looked like turning into a stand-off, but suddenly Bob's hand appeared in between us. 'I'll hang on to that,' he said. 'Until the job's done.'

He reached across and twitched the notes away from Scally. A second later, Scally and I were shaking hands on the deal.

16

I DIDN'T EVEN think of asking Steff about using her wheel. It was no good to her, after all. And I was fixing *her* bike for nothing. She would never know if I swapped her wheel for the one on Scally's bike.

Next day gave me the perfect chance. Bernadette—the aid worker at the sports centre—was starting up a 'school' for the little kids. Justin was desperate to get Taco into it—and that was the very first morning. That meant I could go up to Steff's on my own, while she was taking Pierre to school.

I took Scally's wheel with me and the moment I reached Steff's barn, I went into lightning mode. I took the good wheel off her useless bike and replaced it with the buckled one from Scally's wreck. Then I went to find a hiding place for the good wheel.

I didn't dare take it down the track, in case I met Steff on her way home, so I hid it on the slope opposite the barn—the way Paige and I had come when we first discovered the house. And by the time Steff arrived, I was hard at work on her bike.

She came into the barn and watched me for a while, but she was concentrating on the bike I was mending, of course. She didn't notice the buckled wheel on the other one. I didn't think she ever would—unless she tried wheeling that bike. And why would she do that? I'd already told her it was past repair.

At midday I made a big deal of saying goodbye, pointing at the sun and rubbing my belly to show I had to go back and eat. She waved me off and I cycled away down the track and out on to the road.

But when I was halfway down the hill, I hid my bike in some bushes and doubled back into the woods, working my way back to the slope above the barn.

At the top of the slope I stopped, checking out the yard. If Steff was standing there looking straight up into the woods, she might just have been able to see me. But she wasn't. It was all clear. I started moving forward slowly, ready to creep down and collect the wheel.

Suddenly an arm from behind came snaking round my throat.

'Don't even *think* about it,' growled a voice in my ear. 'Those chickens have got *our* name on them.'

I'd forgotten about the chicken thieves and their camp in the woods. I should have been watching out for them. How was I going to get out of this one?

I nodded hard, to show him I understood. His fingers tightened for a second and he put his mouth closer to my ear.

'Right. I'm going to take my hands away,' he said. 'But don't try anything clever. I'm bigger than you. And faster.'

I nodded again and his hands slid slowly off my neck. 'OK. On your way,' he said. 'Run.'

I turned round and looked at him. He'd been telling the truth. He *was* bigger than me. A tall, dumb-looking kid, with a fuzzy chin and dirty fair hair. I really wanted to do what he said, and run away.

But if I did, I wouldn't be able to fix Scally's bike that day. And suppose this kid found my wheel and walked off with it. What would I do then?

I made myself look him in the eye. 'I'm not after chickens,' I said.

'No?' He looked startled. 'If it's not chickens, what is it?'

'A—a wheel,' I stuttered.

'A wheel?' He leaned closer and peered at me. Then he laughed. 'Hey—you're that boy that mends bikes! And your dad's the gardener.'

'He's not my dad,' I said.

He rubbed the end of his nose, as if it helped him to think. 'I thought you lot were friends with that French woman,' he said. 'But you've got your own little racket going. Where's this wheel?'

I nodded down at the slope.

He took his hands away and gave me a push. 'Fetch it—and then get out of here. And you'd better keep your mouth shut about seeing me. Or I might not be so friendly next time.'

He stood and watched as I slithered down to the clump of bushes. When I came back with the wheel, he grinned scornfully.

'Doesn't look much of a haul. Give me a chicken any day.'

He clapped me on the back, as if we were friends. That was worse than having his hands round my throat. *I'm not like you*, I wanted to say. *This isn't really stealing.* But I knew he wouldn't believe me.

I threaded my arm through the wheel and rode home one-handed. I was a bit anxious about what Justin would say when he saw me, but he was busy cooking and he didn't look up.

'Put that bike away and wash your hands,' he said. 'And next time—tell me where you're going before you disappear.'

He didn't look at me because he was trying to keep

his temper. He hated being angry. Normally that annoyed me, but today it was perfect. I pushed my bike into the tent and hid the spare wheel under my bed.

The only person who saw was Taco. When I straightened up, he was standing in the doorway of the tent, watching what I was doing. He opened his mouth to ask me about it—and I knew Justin would hear what he said. So I put a finger on my lips, as fast as I could.

'Sssh!' I whispered.

A grin spread over Taco's face and he nodded hard. 'Sssh!' he whispered back, and I knew I was safe.

He loves keeping secrets.

After we'd eaten, I cleaned up Steff's wheel and fitted it into Scally's front forks. Then I mended a couple of punctures, oiled the chain and polished the whole bike until it shone.

When Scally turned up the next day, he didn't even recognize the bike. I caught him sneaking a look behind the tent, wondering what I'd done with it.

'It's here,' I said, hauling it out of the tent. 'Cleaned up well, hasn't it?'

'Not bad,' Scally said. He was trying not to look impressed. And failing. 'I'll take it now, shall I?'

'I'd like the money first,' I said.

He loped off to fetch Bob and then grabbed the bike and rode off down the field, grinning all the way. When Bob handed the money over, I understood the grin.

I'd done at least four hours work on that bike and the money I got was just enough to buy one bowl of rice. The same as we'd given Amy for less than an hour. So repairing cycles wasn't as good as being a nurse.

'I got you the best deal I could,' Bob said. 'And remember—this is only the beginning. Scally's got friends and I think you'll have more work coming in soon.'

When he'd gone, I looked at the money and wondered what to do with it. If I spent it on food, it wouldn't last five minutes. I wanted something better for all the work I'd done.

How much would I need to buy a phone?

If I had one, I could call Mum without asking Justin. And I could text my friends too. I really missed that. In my dreams, I kept hearing the *ping* of texts coming in and sometimes it actually woke me up. I'd find myself fumbling around, poking Taco in the face as I searched for the phone.

I stared at the notes for a moment and then I stashed them away in the inside pocket of my backpack. It wasn't much, but it was a start.

Next morning, I was up at the tap stands, waiting to fill the bucket, when a kid came up and nudged me from behind.

'You the one that fixes bikes?' he muttered.

I turned round—and thought, *I know that face.*

It was the chicken rustler. The one who'd grabbed me when I was getting Steff's wheel. He recognized me too, and his mouth opened into a big grin, like a dog's.

'Thought it was you,' he said.

'You a mate of Scally's?' I said. 'What do you want?'

'Scally's got another bike for you to fix. Shall I bring it up to your tent?'

'If you like.' I didn't want to sound too keen. 'Know where we are?' He shook his head, so I pointed down the hill. 'Go through that gate, beside the woman making flatbreads' (that was Muriel) 'and turn right along the top row of tents. When you get to the knife-sharpener—he's easy to spot—turn left down the hill, past the patch of mud where the kids play football. We're in the fifth tent on the right, next to a woman with a sewing machine.'

'OK,' said the boy. 'I'll be down.' He turned away—and then turned back again. 'My name's Wardle,' he said. 'Good to meet you.' He plunged off down the hill, towards the gap in the fence.

It turned out Wardle wasn't on his own. When I got back to the tent, there were three of them there. Him and Scally and another boy as well—much shorter and very *clean*, with dark hair slicked flat and a grey shirt and trousers. I recognized him straight away. He was the one who'd pulled the leg off the chicken. Scally called him Nobo.

They're raiders, I thought. *I'm working with raiders.*

The bike Wardle had brought was even worse than the one before. It needed new tyres and brake pads and a total paint job. Plus, it was too small for any of them—and it was obviously French.

I knelt down and checked it over.

'It's worse than the other one,' I said. 'Cost you more.'

'How much?' Nobo said sharply. His eyes were black and very bright and I knew he was going to haggle me down, whatever I said.

I was just going to pull a number out of the air— maybe ten times what I'd settle for—when a voice spoke from behind me.

'That's my department. Let me talk to Matthew and then I'll give you a price.' And there was Bob, with his hands in his pockets, beaming at them all.

Nobo pulled a face. He knew he wasn't going to have things all his own way if Bob was involved and he didn't like that. But Scally laughed.

'I see you got your own manager, Matt.'

Bob clapped him on the back. 'That's right. Let's go to my tent and sort it out. OK if we leave the bike with you, Matthew?'

He led them away and I went on looking the bike over, working out what I needed to fix it. Making a list in my head, as if Steff's barn was a cycle shop. *Brake pads, gear cables, front light . . .*

'I'm going up to Steff's,' I said, as soon as we'd eaten.

Taco bounced up straight away. 'I'll come too! I want to see Pierre!'

I'd forgotten about it being Saturday. It didn't much matter, though. If Taco was inside with Pierre, he wouldn't get in my way. And the things I needed for the bike repairs would slip into my tool roll. I should still have two or three hours on my own in the barn.

But things didn't work out the way I expected. When we walked into the yard, the little dog came racing out to meet us—and so did Paige.

I didn't know she'd taken to visiting Steff on her own. 'What are you doing here?' I said.

'I was hoping I could use Steff's computer. And she said I could.' Paige was very excited. 'Come and see what I've found!'

Taco charged straight into the house, but I wanted to get those spare parts safely stashed away.

'I'll come in a minute,' I said. 'When I've done a bit of work.'

But Paige wasn't having that. She seized my arm and dragged me towards the house. 'If you go in the barn, you won't come out for hours. And this is really worth seeing. I promise.'

Steff was excited too. She grinned when I came in and burbled away for a moment, waving us all towards the computer. Paige reached across to click the mouse.

And there was Lemon Dough. With the journalists' cars milling around next to the sports centre and Bernadette coming out to welcome them all. There was a foreign voice talking in the background, but I couldn't understand a word.

'What's he saying?' I muttered to Paige.

'No idea,' she muttered back. 'I think it's Arabic or something. Just *watch*.'

The camera cut away down the slope, showing tents and mud, and thin people in dirty, worn-out clothes. And then, suddenly—there was Taco, careering down the slope on my bike, with the broken spokes clattering against the rim.

'*Regarde!*' shrieked Pierre joyfully. '*Regarde, Taco! C'est toi!*'

The two of them were sitting side by side on the floor. Pierre reached out and elbowed Taco, so hard he knocked him over. But Taco didn't care. He bounced up again and elbowed Pierre back.

'*Toi!*' he repeated. '*C'est toi.*' And he gave Pierre a thump that sent him rolling sideways.

'No, it's you, Taco,' Paige said. 'So *you* have to say *moi*, not *toi*. Now be quiet and watch.'

It was too late for that. Pierre and Taco were rolling around hysterically, shoving each other and shouting, '*Toi! Moi! Moi! Toi!*', completely ignoring what was on the screen.

But I was watching. Because the camera had zoomed in on the reporter now—and it was the man who'd spoken to me. Salman. He was talking earnestly, turning round to point at the camp behind him.

I couldn't understand a single word he said—but I knew what he *meant*. He looked sad and angry, as if he couldn't bear to see us all living herded together like that. As if it mattered to him.

'Isn't he great?' Paige said. 'He's telling the world about us!'

I could see she was delighted, but I had to force myself to smile back. Because I wasn't thinking about what Salman was telling the rest of the world. I was remembering what he'd told *me*, that day we met.

That's how to keep your self-respect. Do something worthwhile.

I wondered what he would say if he saw me in Steff's barn, taking spare parts off her bikes? Was that *worthwhile?*

I felt bad for days after that—but I didn't stop fixing bikes for Scally. It wasn't just the money that kept me doing it. It was the work itself. Because the worst thing about Lemon Dough wasn't hunger or thirst or cold.

It was BOREDOM.

There was no TV, no computers, no phones, no games, no books—nothing. If you weren't careful, you ended up just sitting around in the cold. Or going up to the sports centre and squashing in with everyone else—with little kids running all over you and peeing on the floor.

If you had a job, it did more than keep you busy. It marked you out from everyone else. Made you special. Some people even worked for nothing, like the people who taught in the school.

And Muriel.

Everyone knew her, because of the flatbread she made. 'You don't need to pay me,' she always said. 'Just bring your flour and some fuel for the stove.

Cooking your bread keeps my baby warm.'

There was always a long line of people outside her tent. They hung around, waiting for their bread to be cooked, and they kept Charlotte amused as well. Every time I went through the gate by Muriel's tent, I could hear her giggling.

After they brought me the second bike, Scally and his mates discovered that was a good place to be. Whenever they came into the camp, they ended up huddled round Muriel's stove, with Wardle gazing down at her like a great, soft puppy. If I needed to find them, I always looked there first.

That's what I was doing the day Muriel thought of the bonfire.

17

I'D DONE QUITE a few bikes for Scally by then. The latest one had a chain that was past saving. I'd tried to mend it, by taking some links from one of Steff's bikes, but that was no use. I needed to tell Scally he'd have to find a replacement. So I strolled up to Muriel's to see if he was there.

I just made it in time. He was sitting by the stove with Wardle and Nobo, but there were half a dozen other people waiting—people who'd actually brought flour and wood—and Muriel was giving Scally and his mates the push.

She shoved at Wardle's arm, to get him to shift, and he looked down and shook his head at her, like a miserable great walrus. 'You want to get yourself a bigger fire, Muriel,' he said. 'With room for everyone.'

'Oh, brilliant!' Muriel said sarcastically. 'I can really

fit one in here, can't I?' She waved her arm at the tents crammed in around hers.

Nobo rubbed his forehead. 'You could make one on the other side of the gate—on that patch where the kids play football. If you had a bonfire there, it might dry up some of the mud.'

Wardle licked his big, wet lips. 'If you had a bonfire, we could cook potatoes in the ashes.'

'Boy scout!' Scally said scornfully.

But Muriel liked the idea. 'Hey! If we had a *big* bonfire, it would bring people together.'

'Would they let us do it?' I said. Thinking of the soldiers. And the aid workers.

'We won't tell them!' Muriel said. She looked at Scally. 'Pass the word round—but *quietly*. One day next week, I'll wash my red shirt and hang it up on the tent. That's the signal. As soon as it's dark, people should come to the football patch, with the food they want to cook. And some wood for the fire.'

'Can anyone come?' Wardle said.

Muriel laughed and reached up to tug his ear. 'Yes— you too. As long as you bring something with you.'

Wardle looked at her as if she'd just saved the world.

When I told Justin, he loved the idea.

214

'There are plenty of potatoes up at Steff's,' he said. 'I know she'll give us a few to bake in the fire. And she's got lots of wood too. She might let us have a couple of logs.'

She gave us a whole bagful—and that was great, because firewood was short anyway. And it was even harder to find when people started hunting for extra, to take to the bonfire.

They had to hunt stealthily, of course, to avoid awkward questions. Some of them went out in the dark, after the gates were locked, slipping through the hole in the bottom fence. Other people strolled round town in the daytime, watching out for empty cardboard boxes and broken crates.

The wood came into the camp in all sorts of ways—tossed over the fences or pushed underneath them, hidden in backpacks or down people's trouser legs. And it was stashed away behind tents and under camp beds, or dropped into the line of weeds along the fence.

The aid workers knew something was up, of course. Especially Bernadette. She spent a lot of time walking round the camp and chatting, trying to pick up clues and everyone smiled and talked to her, because she was popular. But nobody told her about the bonfire.

The soldiers started patrolling the road, driving up and down to guard the long piles of logs stacked up along the verges. They couldn't guard the forest though. Every scrap of loose wood disappeared—carried into the camp and hidden away.

The day before the bonfire, Bob came in to pay me for the last bike I'd fixed for Scally. As I took the money, he said, 'He'll have another one for you soon.'

'Good!' I said. I'd found a woman in the top field who sold second hand phones. But I hadn't saved up enough money to buy one yet.

'Lots of people fancy having a bike,' Bob said. He glanced over my shoulder, into the tent. 'You want to be careful, Matt.'

'What do you mean?' I looked round, to see what had caught his eye. And there was my own bike, propped opposite the stove.

Bob saw I'd understood. 'You need to look out for yourself,' he said. 'Especially while the bonfire's going on. There'll be lots of people crashing around this field, in the dark.'

'But they'll be people from Lemon Dough,' I said. 'Surely they wouldn't—'

Bob shook his head at me. 'Safer not to trust anyone,' he said.

When he'd gone, I stood and looked at the bike. Suddenly the walls of the tent seemed very flimsy. It wasn't a proper home. Anyone could walk into it and take our things.

I want a real house, I thought. *The way things used to be.*

I undid the padlock and wheeled the bike out of the tent. Then I went back to fetch my tools. Better to take those too. I was just pulling the tool roll out from under the bed when Taco came trailing down the hill and into the tent. He'd been at 'school' and he looked very tired. He glanced into the tent and frowned.

'*Où il est, Papa?*' he said.

'What?' I said. I straightened up, with the tools in my hand. '*What* did you say?'

Taco looked puzzled and suddenly I understood. He'd said those words automatically—*because he was starting to think in French*. As if he belonged here.

I stood up and glared at him. 'If you can't talk properly, just *shut up*! Otherwise you'll turn into a *horrible little French boy*!'

His face crinkled up and he started to cry. I couldn't believe he'd collapsed so easily. I was still angry, but I made myself hug him. That didn't stop him crying. He sat down on the bed and pulled the blanket round his shoulders.

'What's the matter?' I said.

Taco caught his breath. 'Don't feel very well,' he mumbled.

'Do you want Justin?'

He nodded.

'Stay there,' I said, 'and I'll go up to Steff's and fetch him.'

Taco nodded again, wearily, and put his head on the pillow.

I put the tools on the back of my bike and cycled up to Steff's. And while Justin was putting the gardening tools away I took my bike and the tool roll into the barn and hid them right at the back, where no one would see them.

Just till the bonfire was over.

When Justin and I got back to the camp, Taco was fast asleep, looking pink and hot.

'Probably coming down with a cold,' Justin said. 'Sleep's the best thing for him. Let's leave him there.' He started emptying out his pockets. 'Look what Steff's given us for the bonfire. Three *huge* potatoes!'

He'd got them just in time. The next afternoon, Muriel hung out her shirt—and the bonfire just happened. It was like calling up a flash mob. As soon as it grew dark, people picked up their wood and headed for the football patch.

We were right at the front. Taco was still feeling poorly, so Justin carried him up the hill and I took our bundle of wood and the three potatoes. Muriel was ready for us all. She'd marked out the bonfire site with a circle of stones and as the wood arrived she heaped it inside the circle. It went up high and solid and she had Scally and his mates screwing up old newspapers they'd scavenged and pushing them into the gaps.

By the time the soldiers realized something big was happening, they were too late to stop it. Half a dozen of them came marching down the hill towards us, but the bonfire was built by then. And Muriel was standing next to it with a long, lighted stick in her hand.

'Watch out!' someone yelled. 'It's the army.'

'Too bad!' Muriel shouted. She pushed her stick into the middle of the pile and the paper flared up, licking round the wood until it crackled and caught. A roar of delight went up from all round the fire and the soldiers stopped halfway down the slope and waited to see what was going to happen.

It doesn't sound much, does it—a bonfire? But it was the most exciting thing that had happened in Lemon Dough. Until then, we'd been waiting for other people to bring us things. Waiting for water. Or food vouchers. Or news.

But the bonfire was different. We'd done it ourselves—and we weren't going to let the soldiers stop us. So we moved closer together, shoulder to shoulder, forming a solid circle round the fire. The soldiers looked at us for a moment and then went back up the hill.

And everyone cheered.

The night was very still then. The smoke went straight up towards the stars and sparks streamed out of the wood like fireworks erupting in the darkness. At first the fire wasn't right for cooking, of course, but no one minded. It was enough to sit there and feel the heat, to be really, properly *warm*. We all settled down in a huge circle, twenty or thirty deep, talking and telling jokes.

And then the singing started.

It began with someone on the far side of the fire, singing 'The Wheels on the Bus' to a couple of children, but soon everyone was joining in. We sang 'You'll Never Walk Alone', 'Bohemian Rhapsody' and 'All You Need is Love'. And then Kara started on a song I didn't know.

'I'm sitting in a railway station
Got a ticket to my destination . . . '

Muriel caught her breath, but I didn't realize why until Kara reached the chorus. Suddenly she wasn't singing alone any more.

'Homeward bound, I wish I was
Homeward bound.
Home, where my thought's escaping,
Home, where my music's playing,
Home . . . '

Those people who didn't know the words kept quiet and listened, and I could see some of them crying.

Taco was snuggled in between me and Justin, in the row nearest the fire. He'd brought his shoebox, because that was what he liked to hold when he didn't feel well. It was on his lap, and he was cuddling it and gazing into the flames.

Justin put an arm round his shoulders. 'Are you too hot? Want to go further back?'

Taco shook his head dreamily and went on staring at the fire, leaning sideways against Justin. The flames had died down a bit by then and people were starting to push things into the embers. Potatoes. Turnips. Even those tough corn cobs you can't really eat.

Justin wouldn't let us put our potatoes in. 'Not yet,' he said. 'It's too soon. You don't want them to burn.'

So we held them in our hands, watching the burning wood settle lower and trying to spot the best place to bury them when the fire was ready. We had the red glow in front of us and the warmth of the crowd behind and it was the best moment since we'd left home.

Until the soldiers came down the hill again.

We thought they'd given up and gone back to the sports centre. But they must have gone to ask for more orders, because suddenly they were there again, tramping down the hill in a solid block. There were twenty or thirty of them this time, with helmets and riot shields.

Those people who hadn't come to the bonfire turned out to see what was happening. They followed the soldiers, trailing down through the first two fields and stopping in the gateway above the bonfire. There was a whole crowd of them, blocking the way out of the bottom field.

When the soldiers reached the fire, they started waving their shields and barking out instructions. But it was mostly in French and anyway we couldn't hear properly. So nobody moved.

The leader went on shouting for a few moments and then he said something different. Gave an order. And suddenly they were all marching straight at us. Breaking through the circle and heading for the fire.

They didn't pick their way carefully. They went right over us, stamping their feet down wherever they needed to tread. People were yelling and protesting, but it didn't make any difference. The soldiers kept coming. And coming. And coming.

They went right *over* us.

A heavy boot landed on my leg. I screeched and the soldier looked down and saw Taco cringing away from his other foot. He must have been trying to avoid

Taco, because he lurched sideways—and his foot caught the shoebox instead.

It shot forwards into the fire and hit the top of a big log. The lid fell off and the astronauts and the stegosaurus went flying into the middle of the flames, with Mum's photo on top. And as the fire flared up, something else came tumbling out of the box. Hundreds of long rectangles of paper that glinted in the firelight.

Taco wailed and jumped up, reaching into the air to snatch at them. But as the flames caught them they floated up in the strong, hot draught rising out of the fire—and suddenly I realized what I was watching.

It was *money*. British money. Five pound, ten pound, twenty pound notes, catching fire and darkening as they floated up and away into the dark night sky. Everyone was staring up at them now, but no one tried to catch them. Not even the half-burnt notes with their numbers still showing. There were thousands and thousands of pounds disappearing in front of us, but we all knew it wasn't worth trying to save them. Whatever we rescued wouldn't be enough to buy ointment for our burns.

We watched them flare and blacken, glowing at the edges as they disappeared into the darkness beyond the fire, drifting away down the hill, over the tops of the tents in the bottom field.

It was the soldiers who broke the spell. The leader shouted an order and they came battering into the bonfire with their riot shields, knocking the logs apart and stamping on the embers. Baking potatoes splattered into a dirty mush under their feet and a great yell of rage came from round the circle. It wasn't just the fire that was being ruined. It was *food*.

It looked as though there was going to be a battle. The soldiers were armed, but the people round the bonfire were furious now, ready to make a stand.

Justin scrambled to his feet and picked Taco up. 'Come on!' he shouted. 'We've got to get out of here!'

But we couldn't. We were trapped between the crowd and the soldiers. The only way out was straight ahead, across the ruined, trampled fire, but we couldn't go that way. The soldiers hadn't felt the heat through their army boots, but we were just wearing trainers.

Justin hoisted Taco on to his hip and put his other arm round my shoulders, pulling me close. 'Stay together!' he shouted. 'Hang on to me, Matt!'

I wasn't sure I could. The crowd was moving all the time, surging forward so hard I thought it would knock me off my feet. It felt as though I was going to be knocked forward, into the flames.

And then there was a shout from somewhere completely different. From one of the tents, at the bottom of the slope, a desperate voice yelled up to us.

'Fire!'

For a moment I didn't understand. Of course there was a fire. We'd made it on purpose, hadn't we?

Then there was a burst of light from below us and a different kind of flame shot up into the air. A greedy yellow spike, slicing into the darkness. Justin's arm tensed and I heard him catch his breath.

'The money!' he said. 'It's that wretched money!'

The burning notes were dropping down on to the tents and settling on the ramshackle litter of boxes and half-made shelters that cluttered the spaces in between. The whole camp was full of stuff that was ready to burn. Blankets and papers. Rucksacks and clothing. Fuel for the stoves and precious packets of food.

As soon as people realized what was happening, they turned their backs on the bonfire. Everyone started stampeding down the hill, desperate to reach their own tents and save what they'd managed to bring to Lemon Dough. They plunged straight into the thick, dirty smoke that was billowing up from the tents, knocking each other out of the way in their panic.

Bob appeared beside us, dragging Paige behind him. 'Send the kids up the hill!' he shouted to Justin. 'And let's try and get our stuff.'

Justin nodded and pushed Taco into my arms. 'Get him out of here!' he said. 'Go up to the sports centre—and stay there till I come.'

Taco turned towards me blindly, clutching my neck so hard I thought I would choke. He was very heavy, but I knew I couldn't make him walk. I wrapped both my arms round him and started up the hill with my head down, keeping my eyes on Paige's boots to make sure I didn't lose her.

The soldiers started taking charge. Half of them set off down the hill to deal with the fire. The other half began moving everyone away from the bonfire. They cleared the crowd that was blocking the gate and then got us all moving, marshalling us through the two upper fields towards the sports centre.

All the time, we could smell the smoke from the tents below and hear the terrible crackling noise of the spreading fire.

'Just pray the wind doesn't change,' Paige said grimly.

I shivered, but I didn't have enough breath to say anything because Taco was getting heavier and heavier. And he wasn't holding on properly now, so I had to keep stopping to hoist him up higher.

Paige saw me struggling. 'My turn,' she said, holding out her arms.

'It's all right,' I said. 'I can—'

'Don't be stupid!' Paige snapped. 'Give him to me!' And she pulled Taco away from me.

He let himself be handed over, like a parcel, without reacting at all. What was the matter with him?

226

Why was he so quiet? And why wasn't he moaning about his precious shoebox? I wanted to see how he was, but I didn't dare to stop and look, with all the people coming up behind us. It was better to keep going until we reached the sports centre.

We couldn't get inside, of course. It was crammed as tight as a rush hour train, with people standing shoulder to shoulder in the entrance hall.

'Round the back!' I muttered at Paige.

Everyone else was thinking the same thing, of course. We plodded round the building with the rest of the crowd and—finally—we were able to flop down in the car park, sitting on the cold, hard tarmac to catch our breath and coughing to clear the smoke from our lungs.

Paige had Taco on her lap and for a moment I didn't realize how still he was. Then she frowned and shook his shoulder.

'Taco?' she said.

He didn't really wake up. Just lifted his head for a moment, frowning as if he didn't know where he was. Then dropped it down again and lay still.

'Taco!' I said. '*Wake up!*'

'What's wrong?' Paige said. 'Did he get hit on the head?'

I thought back, trying to remember. The soldiers' boots were thick and heavy, but—no, they hadn't touched Taco. Only his shoebox. 'Maybe he's breathed in too much smoke,' I said.

Paige put a hand on his forehead. 'He's very hot.' She took my hand and laid it in the same place. 'Should we find a doctor?'

'Is there one here?' What would we do if there wasn't? We couldn't carry Taco all the way into town.

Paige passed him across to me. 'I'll go and ask at the gate,' she said.

The soldiers always locked up at sunset and tonight there were half a dozen of them guarding the gate, pushing back people who came too close. Paige wriggled her way to the front and started talking to one of the soldiers, waving her arms around and pointing back at Taco.

I could see it was no use. The soldier shook his head and flapped his hand, telling her to go away. He wasn't even listening properly, because half a dozen other people were jabbering away at him at the same time. Paige didn't give up easily, but in the end her shoulders slumped and she pushed her way back through the crowd.

I sat up. 'What did he say?'

'The doctor's coming, but they don't know when. Maybe tonight, maybe tomorrow. He said to wait here. Should I go and find your dad?'

He's not—

'Yes,' I said. 'But get me some water first. And a bit of rag. Taco's burning hot and I want to wipe his face.'

Paige went off towards the taps and I wondered how she would manage to carry the water. And what could she use for a rag? It would all have been so easy if we were still at home.

But if we were at home Taco wouldn't be lying unconscious in my lap, without a doctor.

In the end, Paige came back with someone else's bucket. She stripped off her own sweatshirt and wrung it out in the water. 'Use this for now,' she said. 'I'll try and find something better when I get back.'

She raced off and I wiped the wet sweatshirt across Taco's face. Then I pulled up his sweater and mopped his body too, to try and cool him down. For a moment I succeeded—and he started shivering. Then he was hot again.

I was very frightened. I had no idea what was wrong with him. But I knew he was ill. Really, really ill.

It seemed like a week before Paige came back up the hill with Justin. He stank of smoke and his face was black with ash, but I'd never been so pleased to see him. He knelt down beside me and felt Taco's forehead.

'What can we do?' I said. 'The doctor won't be here till tomorrow.'

He ran a hand down Taco's cheek. 'We've got to get him under cover. It's going to rain tonight and our tent's a wreck. But I don't know where—'

'Bob's sorting that,' Paige said. 'He's going round all the tents in the other fields, to see who's got room for us.'

But we didn't need to wait for Bob. Ten minutes later, Muriel came panting up the hill, with Charlotte in her arms. Her face was blotched and filthy—I think she'd been crying—but she hadn't come for sympathy.

'Get Taco down to our tent,' she said. 'Before the rain starts. He's welcome to my bed. I'm not going to sleep tonight anyway. Quick—before it rains.'

Justin lifted Taco off my lap and we all went down the hill. We tucked Taco into Muriel's bed and the rest of us sat on the floor together, listening to the rain hammering down on the roof of the tent. Waiting for morning. And the doctor.

18

IT WAS ELEVEN o'clock by the time he arrived. By then, there was a huge crowd waiting to see him. He drove through the gates in a battered old car and the moment he stepped out he disappeared as everyone raced forward, calling out for attention.

Justin was there, with Taco in his arms, but there were dozens of other children waiting too. Children with burns, and red eyes and bleeding noses. Some who were wheezing and gasping for breath. Others who couldn't stop coughing.

The doctor was an old man and he looked tired before he started. The soldiers pushed people back and cleared a space in front of the room that was used as a clinic. They tried to organize people into an orderly queue, but everyone was desperate and the line kept collapsing.

It was afternoon before we got Taco inside. By that time, the doctor was totally exhausted. He examined Taco quickly, feeling his forehead and lifting his eyelids to shine a light into his eyes. Taco twitched away from the light, but apart from that he was horribly still.

The doctor sighed wearily and started firing questions at Justin. 'The little boy—was he close to the fire?'

'Very close,' Justin said.

'He was trying to rescue toys, perhaps? From his bed?'

'His bed?' Justin frowned for a moment—and then he understood. 'No, not *that* fire. Taco didn't go down to the tent. He was by the bonfire.'

The doctor shook his head, not really taking in the difference. 'He often has trouble breathing?'

'No,' Justin said. 'Never.'

'So last night—he breathed in a lot of smoke? Yes? Like all the others. And now he can't breathe?' The doctor had obviously decided that was the problem. He started scribbling something on a piece of paper.

Justin was ready to agree with him, but I wasn't. 'It's *not* the smoke,' I said. 'Taco was ill before that. He's been very hot for the last couple of nights. And he wasn't feeling well yesterday. That's why he had the shoebox at the bonfire.'

232

'So what *is* wrong with him?' Justin said desperately.

It was Paige who remembered the rat bite. She asked the doctor a question, in quick, spiky French, and his eyes snapped suddenly. He took off the dressing on Taco's hand and studied the bite. It looked fine, but he shook his head and felt Taco's forehead again. Then he threw away the first piece of paper and wrote on another one. We could see him frowning.

'What is it?' Justin said frantically.

The doctor rattled off something to Paige, in French. Then he shrugged and moved on to the next child.

Paige was frowning too. 'He can't be sure without a blood test, but he thinks it's rat bite fever.'

'So what do we do?' Justin said. 'Where's the hospital?'

Paige shook her head. 'It's different here. You have to pay for things first and then claim it back from your insurance. And the blood test's only a beginning. If it is rat bite fever, Taco needs penicillin, or—'

'Or what?' I said.

'Or he might die.' Paige swallowed. 'The doctor said, *These undernourished children—their resistance is low.*'

We all looked down at Taco. He was very pale now, as if he was dissolving away in front of our eyes.

'So—is the doctor going to give him some penicillin?' Justin said.

Paige sighed. 'There was a supply here, a couple of weeks ago. But it's all been used and the aid agencies haven't sent any more. I think there's a shortage everywhere. The doctor's given you a prescription for penicillin, in case you can find some. But you'd have to pay for that too.'

'He knows we haven't got any money!' Justin said desperately. 'That's why we're here. If we had money—'

'I've got some money!' I said. At last there was something I could *do*! 'I got paid for mending those bikes. I'll go and get—'

And then I saw the expression on Justin's face.

'Oh Matt,' he said. 'Was it in the tent?'

I couldn't believe the money was all gone. I'd worked so hard to earn it and I'd put it away so carefully—in the inside pocket of my backpack, hidden away right under the camp bed. It *must* still be there.

Justin saw me look down the hill. 'Don't—' he said.

But I had to. I ran down the hill, through the first gate, across the middle field and past Muriel's tent. She called out to me, but I didn't even hear what she said. I just went through the gate and kept on running.

The bonfire was still smouldering on the football patch. The soldiers had damped it down with earth, but I could feel the heat coming off it as I ran past.

The row of tents immediately below it was almost untouched and I started hoping, even though I could smell the stink of the embers ahead. *Maybe . . .*

And then I reached the next row. And I saw.

Everything below me was ruined. There was nothing left except heaps of wet black ash, littered with twisted tent poles and melted plastic buckets. One or two people were wandering around, stirring the ash with their feet, but there was nothing left to find.

I walked down the slope to where our tent should have been, counting the rows to make sure I got it right. Just in case our tent was different from all the others. In case something had survived.

But there was nothing.

The fabric of the tent had shrivelled away and the ground was covered with thick, foul soot. The camp beds were empty frames and underneath mine—the one I'd shared with Taco—I could see the remains of a zip and some twisted plastic buckles.

I crouched down and touched them. The zip was still hot enough to hurt but I pulled it away and there, underneath, was one tiny coin, bent and discoloured from the heat. A single cent. All that was left of my hard-earned money.

A hand came down on my back and I thought Justin had followed me.

'It's not *fair*!' I said bitterly. 'I worked for days to earn that money and now it's gone—and we *need* it. Taco's *got* to have penicillin.'

'Don't give up,' said Bob's voice. 'There might be a way to get some.'

I stood up slowly and turned round to look at him. 'What do you mean?'

'There's a shortage of penicillin,' he said slowly. 'Right across Europe. But I've got—contacts. You know how people in the haulage business get around. They might be able to lay their hands on some for you.'

'But what about money?' I said. 'Wouldn't we have to pay for it?'

Bob looked at me, as though he was working something out. 'They might do a trade,' he said slowly. 'If you go and collect the stuff. I don't think they'll deliver, with petrol the price it is.' He glanced round at the wreckage of our tent. 'Doesn't look as though your bike was in the fire.'

Thank goodness, I thought. 'I took it up to Steff's. Like you said.'

'You're a sensible kid,' Bob said. He grinned suddenly and clapped me on the arm. 'Why don't you go up and collect it? And I'll make a phone call or two and see what I can set up.'

'That's great!' I could hardly believe it. 'Justin's going to be so grateful. I'll just go and tell him—'

'I can do that,' Bob said cheerfully. 'You get on and fetch the bike. The sooner you get yourself on to the road, the quicker Taco's going to have his penicillin.'

He was right, of course. There was no time to waste. I nodded and hurried down the field, towards the gap in the fence. When I was through, I glanced back and saw Bob climbing the slope, with his phone to his ear. It looked as though he wasn't wasting time either.

I meant to grab the bike out of Steff's barn and leave, straight away. But when I reached the house the little dog started barking—of course—and Steff came out and grabbed me. She pointed up towards Lemon Dough and gabbled something I didn't understand.

'*Le feu! Le feu!*'

Then she shook my shoulder and fired off a whole stream of questions, as if she had to ask them, even though she knew it was pointless. When I shook my head—to show I didn't understand—she frowned for a moment, struggling for words.

Then she pointed at me and said, 'OK? Yes?'

I nodded because that was the easiest thing to do. Then I tried to move away, but she hadn't finished.

'Justin—OK?' she said.

Then I realized what was going on. She knew about the fire. And she wanted to be sure we were all right.

I nodded again, to let her know about Justin, and thought, *Please stop there. Please don't ask any more.* But she did, of course.

'Taco—OK?'

I nearly lied. I nearly nodded again, just to make her let go of me. But she could see the answer from my face and she knew something was wrong. So out came another huge stream of words that didn't make any sense to me.

She wasn't going to let me go until I'd told her about Taco. Maybe she even thought he was dead. But I couldn't explain what was wrong. I couldn't even tell her that I had to leave, straight away, to have any chance of putting it right.

I thought I would have to hit her, just to make her let go of me. But then, in the nick of time, Paige came slithering out of the forest, sliding down the slope opposite the barn.

'Bob's found some penicillin!' she shouted. 'He's drawn you a map, to show where you have to go.'

Steff whirled round, rattling off her questions at Paige instead. When she heard the answers, she let out a huge gasp. Then she ran into the barn, beckoning us to follow her. When we went through the door, she was unlocking her best bike, the one I'd mended.

'I don't need that,' I said. 'I've got my own bike.'

But she wasn't giving it to me. She pushed it at

Paige, saying something in a fierce, insistent voice. Waving her hand and pointing up the road. And Paige nodded and took the bike.

'What is it?' I said. 'What's she doing?'

'She's telling me to go with you,' Paige said. 'And she's right. You'll never manage on your own. Not if you need to talk to people. Come on. Let's get going.' And she jumped on to the bike and started pedalling down the track.

19

THAT CAUGHT ME off balance. Was Paige going back to Lemon Dough? I knew I ought to do that, to tell Justin about the penicillin. But if Paige was setting off straight away I had to go with her—because she had the map.

Steff gave me a push. '*Vite! Vite, vite vite!*' she said.

I didn't understand—but I could see what she meant. *Hurry up! Get going!* I nodded and started cycling after Paige, as fast as I could.

She was a good cyclist. I didn't catch up with her until she was out on the road—heading away from Lemon Dough. Then I put on a desperate sprint, pedalling flat out until our bikes were side by side.

'Hang on,' I panted. 'Need to stop—look at—map.'

'*I* know where we're going,' Paige said impatiently. But she pulled into the side of the road and took a folded piece of paper out of her pocket. 'We have to get to a town called Angoulême, about eighty kilometres away. Look, here's the route.'

I was too hassled to take it in properly. What she had wasn't a proper, printed map. It was just a rough sketch covered in French names, full of 'x's and *Le* and *La* and *Les*. At the bottom, Bob had written an address in Angoulême. And a name. *Victor Masson.* Above that, lines went left and right all the way to the top of the paper.

'I'll never remember all that,' I said.

Paige shook her head. 'You don't need to. It's a list of places really. As long as we can find those, we'll get there. Look—the first one's *Le Vieux Moulin.* When we get there we have to turn left.' She pushed the map into her pocket and set off again. What could I do except follow her?

After half an hour there was no sign of the *Vieux Moulin,* so we laid our bikes down at the side of the road and had another look at the map. Bob must have drawn it very quickly and he'd only put in the roads we had to follow. If we'd missed our turn, we were lost.

'He's sending us on the little roads,' Paige said. 'He thought it would be quicker that way, on bikes.' She ran her finger along the line Bob had drawn. '*Watch the signposts and you'll be OK*, he said.'

I frowned down at the map. 'We *must* be nearly at *Le Vieux Moulin*.'

Paige grinned as she picked up her bike. 'That's the first thing I've ever heard you say in French. Great accent!' She pedalled off before I could shout at her.

We cycled for another hour, checking every sign-post we passed, but there was no sign of the wretched Moulin place. And then the rain started coming down. We hadn't got any extra clothes, so there was nothing to do except pedal harder, to try and keep warm.

Soon we were soaking wet—and beginning to realize we were lost.

We came down into a small town called something like Ruffaud, with a river running through the middle. Paige pulled up in the main square and got off her bike.

'This is hopeless,' she said. Dripping all over the pavement. 'We need to ask someone, before the shops all close. Hang on to this.'

She pushed her bike at me and marched into the nearest shop. The window was full of beautiful, delicate cakes, like food from a fairytale. Beyond those, in the shop, a brisk woman in an overall was wiping down the counter. As Paige walked in, she looked up sharply, first at her face and then down at her feet— and the puddle that was forming on the floor.

Paige smiled politely and I saw her ask a question. The only answer she got was a frown and an impatient shake of the head, but she didn't give up. She asked again, pulling out the map, which was getting very soggy. Unfolding it carefully, she spread it out on the counter.

The brisk woman was outraged. The cloth trembled in her hand and I thought she was going to wipe it across the counter again and knock the map to pieces. Then she condescended to bend over and look at it. She pulled a horrified face—a *Well, you don't want to be HERE!* look—and started talking very fast, pointing and waving her arms about.

The good thing was that she made sure Paige knew exactly where we had to go. I could see her saying it over and over again, like a magic spell, until Paige was word perfect. As soon as she'd got it, there was another brisk nod. *OK—on your bike!*

Paige raced out of the shop, grabbed her bike and jumped on to it. Before I could ask what had happened, she was riding back over the bridge, at top speed.

'Wait!' I shouted.

But she didn't. She didn't even look round. All I could do was pedal after her, going back the way we'd come. She didn't stop until she reached the sign on the edge of the town. When I caught up with her she was swearing very loudly, in English and French, and kicking it as hard as she could.

She didn't stop when I pulled up beside her. The swearing went on for another ten seconds or so, until she ran out of breath. Then there was a dodgy moment, when I thought she might burst into tears.

'If it wasn't so awful, it would be *funny*,' she said bitterly. 'If only it didn't *matter* so much.'

'We've gone the wrong way?' I said.

'We're miles and miles away from Le Vieux horrible Moulin. The cake woman said we'd have to miss it out and go—' And she rattled off a long French rigmarole.

'Hope *you* understand that,' I said.

Paige nodded wearily. 'It means we have to take the next right turn and then go right again when we hit the main road. The cake woman said that was the only sensible way.'

'Better get going then,' I said. 'We've lost a lot of time. We'll have to cycle through the night.'

Paige looked up. The sky was darkening very fast. 'No lights on this bike,' she muttered.

I didn't waste time thinking about that. Just pedalled off down the road, looking for the next right turn.

Within an hour it was almost completely dark. The darkest dark I'd ever seen. There were always street lights at home and Lemon Dough had floodlights all round the sports field. But here—there was nothing.

We blundered along small, twisting roads, through villages where all the houses were dark, even though it was only ten at night. We didn't see any proper lights until we finally reached the main road.

Then suddenly there were lots. Red ones and white ones. All moving.

The road was lit by a steady stream of trucks thundering along in both directions. I cycled straight up to the junction and I was just going to pull out on to the road when Paige came up behind me and grabbed at my fleece.

'Do you want to die?' she said.

I tried to shake her off. 'Look—we've got to get on. We've lost too much time already.'

'It won't help Taco if you get squashed by a lorry,' she said tartly. 'Use your brains. I know you've got lights, but those lorries aren't going to see you, Matt. Not on a road like this. And I won't stand a chance, will I? I'll get flattened like a hedgehog.'

For a split second I thought, *I'll go on my own, then*. If I cycled through the night I'd be in Angoulême first thing in the morning. And once I was there I could show the address to people and let them point the way. I didn't need to wait for Paige.

Only—

Now she'd made me stop, I'd had a chance to look at the road. And I could see she was right. It would be foolish to be out on that in the dark, even if I did have lights.

'What shall we do?' I said.

Paige pointed along the verge. 'It's pretty wide there. We could shelter in the bushes and we might even get some sleep. Then we can set off again, as soon as it's light.'

We heaved the bikes along to the widest part of the verge and worked our way into a clump of bushes that was growing up against a fence. There was nothing behind the fence except a dark patch of trees, so once we'd made a space in the bushes we were completely hidden.

It was cold and damp and uncomfortable, but there was nowhere else to go. We leaned back against the fence and Paige took some of Muriel's flatbread out of her pocket.

'Iron rations,' she said.

We chewed our way through a couple of pieces and then curled up on the ground and waited for it to get light.

You always sleep a bit, even in terrible places. Even when you're worried sick, and desperate to reach the end of your journey. I thought I'd only closed my eyes for a moment, but when I opened them again everything round us was sopping wet with dew and the sky was a clear, pale grey.

It was four o'clock in the morning. And there was no noise coming from the road.

I leaned over and shook Paige's shoulder. 'Wake up! We ought to go now!'

She groaned and sat up before she was properly awake, blinking and shaking her head from side to side. 'What? It's not—' Then she heard the silence and she nodded. 'You're right. Let's go.'

That was the first time I really saw France.

We set off into the dim, grey morning, with the sun just beginning to rise. Gradually the sky on our right turned pink and the light caught every dewdrop on the grass. We were cycling between glittering verges, past valleys hung with scarves of mist.

The great open fields spread out on either side of us, rolling uninterrupted over the gentle slopes. Sheets of green, broken by patches of woodland and pale stone barns.

It was all so big.

And *beautiful*. I hadn't expected that.

My feet went round and round without needing to be told. The bike flew up and down the hills and I started to feel that things were going to come out right. We'd get the penicillin this morning and by the time it was dark we'd be back in Lemon Dough. And Taco would get better. Everything was going to be fine.

And then Paige got a puncture.

20

SHE'D RACED AHEAD of me, going uphill, and I had my head down trying to catch up. I was almost level when I looked up and saw her at the side of the road, feeling her front tyre.

I knew what was wrong, of course. By the time I reached her, I'd worked out what I was going to do. There was a little picnic area just ahead of us.

'Let's go there,' I said. 'Easier than fixing it by the side of the road.'

I heaved the bike on to one of the picnic tables and spun the wheel. No problem about finding the puncture. There was a big, ugly nail stuck in the tyre. I found my tyre levers and started taking it off. Not hurrying, but working steadily.

A job takes as long as it takes. That was what Grandpa

used to say. *Unless you try and hurry—then it takes twice as long.*

I knew the inner tube was ropey because I'd put half a dozen patches on it already. This new hole was bigger than any of the others and I really needed to take the wheel off and do it properly, with the inner tube on the table. But there wasn't time for that.

I could feel Paige fidgeting beside me, desperate to get going again, so I tried to get her talking. I thought that would be less distracting.

'Your mum's French, isn't she?' I said. 'So why isn't she here with you and Bob?'

There was no answer.

I glanced up and saw Paige looking at me. Our eyes met and she went pink. 'None of your business,' she said gruffly.

What was the big deal? Half the kids in my class have parents who've split up, and some of them have never even seen their dads. They all know where their mums are, though. I was ready to bet Paige knew too.

Maybe her mum was in prison.

I picked up the sandpaper and roughed up the tube around the hole. 'Did she and your dad split up a long time ago?'

Paige picked at the edge of the picnic table. 'He's not my dad,' she said.

It was like listening to myself. 'OK, your step-dad,' I said. I picked up the glue and started spreading it round the hole.

'No,' Paige said. Very carefully and deliberately. 'He's not my step-dad either.' She stopped for a minute. The way people stop when they're deciding whether or not to tell you something. Then she said, 'I'd never even seen him until we all came out of the tunnel.'

I tested the glue with my finger, to see if it was ready. Not yet. 'So why are you both pretending?' I said, without looking at her.

Paige took a long, difficult breath. 'Remember when we were in the cutting? With all those rumours flying around? Bob knew he wouldn't be allowed to stay without a child. So he found me.'

'You were on your own?' I said.

Paige nodded. 'I hitched a ride on a lorry that was going through the tunnel. I think the driver was sorry for me. But Bob told me I wouldn't be allowed to stay on my own. He said we needed each other.'

'So what happened to your parents?'

She banged her fist down suddenly on the table. Very hard. 'They were killed by some filthy scadgers,' she said fiercely.

The glue was tacky. I noticed just in time and I picked up the patch and smoothed it on. Very carefully. Making sure I didn't let it crease in the middle. Then I picked up the chalk and the grater and grated some chalk on top of the patch, until it was covered in fine, white dust. I blew off the loose chalk and started fitting the inner tube back.

'Your parents were raiders,' I said slowly. Watching my fingers as they eased the tube into its place.

Paige lifted her head. 'They were just trying to find some food,' she said. 'What were we supposed to do when the scadgers had emptied all the shops? Starve to death?'

I picked up the tyre and fitted it over the inner tube. 'Some people grew things in their gardens,' I said carefully.

Paige gave an angry little laugh. 'That's difficult when you live in a flat. We couldn't grow anything except carrots in a window box. And my dad lost his job, so we couldn't afford to buy food on the black market.'

'It must have been very hard,' I said. I picked up the pump and started re-inflating the wheel, very slowly and carefully. I wanted her to be quiet. I didn't want to think about what she was saying.

But she wouldn't stop. 'And then, one day, I came down in the morning and there was food for breakfast.

251

That was the first time I went to school without feeling hungry. And there was more food in the evening. I had two whole meals in one day—and there was food in the cupboard as well. It was like magic.'

'You didn't know where it was coming from?'

'Not then. Not until I woke up one night and the house was empty. I was down in the kitchen when they came home with their bags full, so they had to tell me.' Paige looked down at her fingers. 'After that, I used to lie awake in the dark, listening to them go out together. And one night they didn't come back.'

She stopped and looked at me, waiting for me to react.

I could have told her then. About how things had been hard for us too. About why Mum had started swapping and stashing food away. And ScadgePost.

But I didn't. I fitted the cap on the valve and packed my tools away. 'We're losing time,' I said. 'We ought to get going again.'

Half an hour later, we were cycling into Angoulême on a big dual carriageway. Trucks kept thundering past us and it was impossible to stop and look at the map. I turned down the first side street that didn't lead into a retail park and pulled the damp, tattered paper out of my pocket.

Paige dabbed at it with her finger. 'I think we're here,' she said. It was the first time she'd spoken since we left the picnic table. 'We need to go along to here and take that turn, towards the station. Then we go round *there* and look out for this shop.' She bent over, trying to read the words. 'I think it's called Benoît and Landauer. Bob said the yard was next door to that. He said they'd be expecting us.'

'How did he fix it all up?' I hadn't thought of that before, but now it jumped out at me. 'He doesn't speak French.'

'I think they understand English.' Paige lifted her hand off the map. 'I . . . heard him talking to them.'

I thought she was going to say something else, but she didn't, so I took another look at the map, to memorize the route. Then I nodded at her. 'Let's go.'

Ten minutes later we pulled up outside Benoît and Landauer. It was a small, dingy chemist's shop in a back street and next to it was a pair of big wooden gates.

'Is it here?' Paige said uncertainly.

'I think so.' It didn't look much like a haulage yard to me. I got off my bike and put my eye to a crack in the wood. But all I could see was half a dozen bicycles and a couple of dirty white vans.

'There's a bell,' Paige said.

She pressed it and I jumped back quickly as footsteps came towards us across the yard. One of the gates swung open and out came a short, red-faced man, as round and shiny as a beach ball. Big cheeks. Big, bald head. Big muscles in his bare, tattooed arms. The only thing that didn't fit with the beach ball look was the thick black moustache frothing out from his top lip.

Paige started explaining why we'd come, in her polite French voice, but the man didn't bother to listen to that.

'Bob?' he said. His accent made it sound weird. When I nodded, he turned back into the yard, bellowing, 'Victor!'

The second man who appeared was much younger. His face was pale and smooth and he looked us up and down carefully and then beckoned us through the gate.

'Come in quickly,' he said. He had a French voice, but he could speak English all right—faster than anyone I've ever heard. 'So Bob sent you for something important, right? He said you need this for your brother to save him from dying and by good luck—by *great* good luck—we have a small amount of this thing that you need. But you have to remember that we are not millionaires, my father and I. This thing did not come to us for nothing, and we need to be paid so I hope you understand that.'

All the time he was talking, his eyes were flickering over me and my bike, and then over Paige and hers. I tried to catch Paige's eye, but she was staring down at the ground.

'We haven't got any money,' I said. 'Bob told us we could sort that out later.'

'Bob!' Victor said. He laughed, as if that was a good joke. Then he turned round to his father and said it again, in the same voice. 'Bob!' Followed by a whole lot I couldn't understand, in French. And both of them laughed.

Paige pinched her lips together and I saw her fists clench. While Victor was still talking to his father, she took a step towards me and muttered under her breath. 'Bob's set you up. He told them you'd trade your bike for the penicillin.'

'He told them *what?*' I said.

But I knew she was right. As soon as she said it, I saw that it was the only thing that made sense. If there was a shortage of penicillin, nobody was going to hand some over to us for nothing. We had to have something to trade. *I'll think of something*, Bob had said.

And he'd thought of my bike.

When Victor turned back towards us, he wasn't laughing any more. 'The nonsense is finished,' he said briskly. 'You give me the bike and I give you the pills, OK? It's a deal?'

He took a little bottle out of his pocket and held it up in the air for me to see. On the front was a white label that said *Benoît and Landauer* and underneath, in black ink, *penicillin 50*. Inside were dozens of little white tablets. I could see them quite clearly through the brown glass sides of the bottle.

'My brother needs those pills fast,' I said. 'If I give you my bike, how will I get them back to him?'

Victor's eyes flickered. 'Maybe I can drive you back to your camp,' he said. 'But this will take time—and fuel for the van. And I told you before, we are not rich men.' His eyes swivelled round, moving from my bike to Paige's. 'But I will do it—for two bikes.'

Paige flared up at him. 'That wasn't in the deal! Bob didn't know I was coming with Matthew. And anyway, this bike isn't ours. We *can't* give it to you.'

Victor shrugged and started to put the pills back in his pocket.

'Wait!' I said. I looked at Paige. 'If you take the pills, you can cycle back to Lemon Dough. And I'll hitch.'

But Victor was ready for that. 'Ah—no,' he said cheerfully. 'I can't allow such danger. Hitching is not safe for a young man like you. We must drive you back. I insist. *OK, Papa?*'

His father grunted. He leaned back against the big wooden gates folding his arms and grinning at us and I knew we'd never get past him. He was as big as Paige and me put together.

'So?' Victor said. His voice was as smooth as oil now. 'It's decided?'

What could we do?

'Decided,' I said. Quickly, before I could think any more. 'As long as you give me the pills and then take us back straight away.' I held out my hand.

Victor dropped the pills into it and pulled a key out of his pocket. 'Come,' he said. 'You can put the bikes over there.'

He went over and unlocked one of the shabby old vans and we wheeled the bikes to the far side of the yard and leaned them against the wall, with the others. As I let go of mine, my hands hovered over the handlebars, just for a second.

'Come on,' Paige said softly. 'It's only a bike.'

What did she know?

I left it leaning there, in that scruffy, dirty yard and went across to the van. Victor opened the back doors and waved us in. The van was full of junk and old boxes and there was nothing to sit on except the floor. We slithered in and he banged the doors shut and jumped into the cab. Then he reversed out of the yard and we began our bumpy journey back to Lemon Dough.

'What are we going to tell Steff?' I said.

Paige shook her head. 'No use trying to be clever. All we can do is tell her what really happened. If she wants to call the police, that's her business. But we didn't have any choice, did we? *Il faut vivre*. That's what my mother always used to say. You've got to live.'

Il faut vivre. I clutched the pills tightly in my hand, holding them against my chest so that the bottle didn't get broken as we slithered around the back of the van. They were the most important thing. Nothing else really mattered except getting them back to Taco.

It only took Victor an hour to drive us back. He pulled up in the village square, beside the ugly church, and came round to let us out of the van.

'You can walk from here,' he said when he opened the doors. 'It's better for me to stay away from the camp.'

I didn't bother to say anything to him. What was the point? I just jumped out of the van and started running across the square.

It was a bright, clear day and as I came over the top of the hill I saw the whole of Lemon Dough spread out below me. There were still rows of tents in the top two fields, but the bottom field was just a black, empty space. Lines of people were moving slowly across it, clearing the rubble away.

I ran as fast as I could, all the way down the hill. Paige's legs were longer than mine, but she didn't catch me up until we reached the gate. 'Don't kill yourself,' she gasped. 'Ten minutes won't make any difference.'

'It might,' I panted back. 'You don't *know*.'

I raced through the gate and down the first field, heading for Muriel's tent. Once I stumbled and nearly fell over, and the shock almost stopped me breathing. *Suppose I'd broken the bottle . . .* But I was still on my feet, clutching the bottle tightly in my right hand.

At the entrance to Muriel's tent, I paused for a moment, just to catch my breath. Then I ducked inside.

And there was no one there.

21

THE CAMP BED was empty, with the blankets flung on to one side. And Taco's trainers were lying upside down underneath it.

They were the only shoes he had. He wore them all the time.

I stared at them, trying to make sense of what I was seeing. Why didn't Taco need his shoes? Were we too late? I clenched my fingers harder round the bottle, feeling the edge of the cap digging into the palm of my hand. *Taco* . . .

Then Paige said, 'Look—Muriel!'

I turned round and there she was, running down the hill towards us and waving frantically. She looked tense and excited, but not exactly sad. Did that mean—? Maybe—?

'It's all right!' she panted as soon as she was near

enough for us to hear. 'I saw you go past the sports centre, but I wasn't quick enough to catch you. Taco's up there. Bernadette found him a place inside, because he's so ill. Did you get the penicillin?'

I couldn't speak. But I lifted the bottle to show her and she hugged me, hard. 'Brilliant!' she said. 'Well done! Let's get it up to him!'

I couldn't run another step. My legs were shaking and I could hardly breathe. But I started trudging up the hill with Muriel on one side of me and Paige on the other. Muriel was talking away all the time.

'Justin's been worried sick about you. He couldn't leave Taco, but he was desperate to know where you were.'

'Bob was going to tell him,' Paige said.

'Well, he didn't,' Muriel said tartly. 'Justin didn't find out what you were doing, until Steff came up here, to ask if you were back. There was a lot of shouting then. Justin—'

I wasn't interested in that. 'What about *Taco*?' I said. 'Is he getting better?'

Muriel frowned. 'He's still very hot. And he's come out in a weird rash on his hands and feet. Justin got him to drink some water this morning, but he was sick straight away.'

That didn't sound good. 'Is he awake?'

'In a way. But he's not really conscious. He keeps going on and on about the money that fell in the fire.' Muriel ducked round the side of the sports centre. 'He's in a little room at the back here. It was the best they could do.'

It wasn't really a room at all. More of a cupboard, with no window. But there was room for a camp bed with a chair squashed in beside it and Taco was sitting up in the bed with Justin's arm round him. He was sipping at a cup of water.

'Here!' I said. I stood in the doorway and held out the bottle.

'Oh, Matt!' For a terrible moment I thought Justin was going to burst into tears. 'I've been frantic—'

'Yes,' I said. 'I'm sorry. But—look, this is penicillin for Taco. He ought to have some, straight away.'

'Hang on,' Justin said. He leaned over and spoke softly to Taco. 'I'm going to put you down. Only for a minute. Then we'll give you the medicine Matt's brought—and you'll start getting better.'

Taco's eyes flicked open, but I could see they weren't focusing. He was just staring vaguely into nowhere. 'No,' he muttered. 'No, we haven't got the money. I can't—'

'You don't *need* any money,' I said. I caught hold of his wrist as Justin laid him down on the bed. 'Listen, Taco. *It's all right*. You haven't got to buy anything.

These pills have been paid for. All you've got to do is swallow them—and get better.'

Justin was looking at the bottle, turning it round and round in his hands. 'There aren't any instructions on the label. How do I know how much to give him?'

I hadn't even noticed that.

'You'll have to ask someone,' Justin said. 'The doctor's gone. You'd better go and find Amy.'

'Taco ought to have a tablet first.' I opened the bottle and tipped a tablet into the palm of my hand. 'Can he just swallow it?' I said.

Justin shook his head. 'He'd find that really hard. I'll break it up and give it to him in this water.'

He dropped the tablet into the mug he was holding and hammered at it with the end of a pen until it was a fine white dust. Then he put his arm round Taco's shoulders, lifted him up, very gently, and held the mug to his lips.

'Drink this,' he said. 'Take it slowly, so it doesn't make you sick.'

Taco frowned muzzily. Then he closed his eyes and turned his head away.

'You've got to have it,' I said. 'Please, Taco. It's—'

What would make him drink it? There must be something I could say. Something that would make him see—

And then it came to me. I leaned forward and said it loudly and clearly, to make sure he was hearing me. 'You must drink this, Taco. *It cost a lot.* So you mustn't waste it, because there's no more money.'

His eyes flickered open and he looked at me, struggling to focus on my face. 'Really a lot?' he said.

'*Yes,*' said Paige's voice from the doorway. 'That medicine cost Matthew *really a lot*. So you'd better swallow it all.'

Looking very solemn, Taco opened his mouth wide and Justin tipped the mug slowly, pausing after every couple of drops to let him swallow. When it was empty, Taco looked straight at me and gave me a big smile. Then Justin lowered him slowly on to the bed and a moment later, he was asleep.

'Come on,' Paige muttered. 'Let's go and find Amy.'

We ran down the hill to Amy's tent. She must have heard us coming, because she came out to meet us.

'How is he?' she said. 'Any better?'

'I hope so,' I said. 'Look—we've got these.' I handed the bottle to her and she read the label and nodded approvingly.

'That's what he needs. Clever of you to track some down. Where did you find it?'

'It doesn't matter,' Paige said quickly. 'We just need to know how often to give him a tablet.'

Amy gave me a puzzled look. 'It doesn't say on the prescription?'

I'd forgotten about that. 'I think it said three times a day. But—are the tablets always the same strength?'

'I don't understand,' Amy said. 'The pharmacist should have given you what was on the prescription.' She saw me hesitate and her face sharpened. 'You did get these from a pharmacist, didn't you?'

I shook my head.

Amy unscrewed the top of the bottle and held it up to her nose. Then she tipped a tablet into the palm of her hand and sniffed at that.

'What's the matter?' I said. 'What are you doing?'

She handed me the bottle. 'Smell that,' she said. 'Does it remind you of anything?'

I sniffed, carefully. 'It's a bit like . . . vinegar.'

Paige leaned over and smelt it too. 'Is there something wrong with the tablets?'

Amy pulled a face. 'I'm sorry,' she said. And I could see she meant it. 'I'm really sorry—but these tablets aren't penicillin. They're very old aspirin. Starting to deteriorate.'

I couldn't say a word. After all that cycling—and the night by the side of the road—and Victor and his father—and the bike—

No. I mustn't think about the bike.

Everything swirled about in my head and I felt as if I was going to choke. I could see Paige with her eyes burning and her lips thin with fury, but it felt as though she was a million miles away. I couldn't make a sound.

Then Paige grabbed my arm and shook it. 'Don't freeze on me,' she said. 'We can't just give up. We need to *think*.' She looked at Amy. 'Suppose Taco goes on taking that aspirin. Will it do him any harm?'

Amy shook her head. 'Might make his stomach sore, that's all. But it won't do him any *good*.'

'But he *thinks* it will,' Paige said. 'When we gave it to him, he looked better, straight away. Could it make a difference—just because he believes it will?'

'I suppose—it might,' Amy said doubtfully. 'Nobody really knows how that kind of thing works.'

'You mean, we could just carry on giving it to him?' I said.

Amy sighed. 'It's worth a try. But I wouldn't tell Justin about the pills. If he knows they're useless, Taco might pick that up. That's all the advice I can give you.' She hesitated, as if she wasn't quite ready to go.

'I'm sorry,' I said. 'We haven't got anything for you. We lost it all in the fire.'

Her face turned bright red. 'I don't want anything!' she said. 'Taco's a smashing kid. I don't know what lowlife sold you those aspirins—but you make sure he pays for it!' She nodded fiercely and ducked back into her tent.

'Oh, we will,' Paige said softly. 'We certainly will.' She leaned over and took the medicine bottle out of my hand. 'I'm going to give these back to Justin and tell him Amy said three times a day. You wait there. If Justin sees your face, he'll know there's something wrong.'

She disappeared back up the hill and I put my hands up and felt my cheeks. They were burning hot and I knew my face must be redder than Amy's. But I didn't feel angry. I didn't feel anything except—empty.

A couple of minutes later, Paige was back. 'Come on,' she said grimly. 'Let's go and find him.' She strode off and I had to jog to catch up with her.

'Find who?' I said.

'Bob, of course.' She didn't stop walking. 'He's not going to get away with this.'

'It wasn't him,' I said. 'It was the other two. Victor and his dad.'

Paige just laughed—a short, sour laugh.

'You're just guessing,' I said. 'You don't *know*.'

'But I'm going to find out,' Paige said. And she put her head down and went on walking.

It took us an hour to track Bob down. We went round the camp three times without finding him. He wasn't in the sports centre, he wasn't queuing for water or waiting to charge his phone, and he wasn't down in the bottom field raking through the ashes.

In the end, it was Muriel who gave us a lead. 'I saw him half an hour ago,' she said. 'Heading up towards the woods. Maybe he was going to see the boys. Why?'

Paige didn't answer. She just turned round and headed down the hill towards the gap in the fence. I hurried after her.

'Remember—it might not have been his fault,' I said. 'Maybe he didn't know they were going to give us aspirin.'

'We'll soon know,' Paige said. 'Filthy scadger.' She squeezed through the gap and marched out on to the road without even looking behind to see if I was following.

Bob was with Scally and Nobo and Wardle, sitting round their fire and chewing on some kind of meat. When we came crashing through the trees, he jumped up and held out his hands.

'Did you get it?' he said. 'Has Taco started taking it?'

Paige glared at him. 'Murderer!' she said.

Bob snatched at her wrists, holding her away from him. What have I done?'

'It was aspirin!' I shouted. 'They took my bike—and Steff's—and they gave us *aspirin*!'

'Those villains!' Bob said heavily. 'I've worked with Victor for fifteen years. And he ripped you off?' He shook his head. 'I'm shocked rigid.'

But I could see he wasn't. The answer came out too fast. As if he'd had it ready all the time.

'You *knew*!' I said. 'You let them give us fake penicillin, because you thought we'd never find out.'

'But we did,' Paige said. 'So you'd better tell them to bring those bikes back.'

Bob gave a quick snort of laughter. 'You're not living in the real world. There's no way—'

'You're the fixer,' said Paige. 'So—fix this—*Mr Super-Scadger*.' She wrenched her wrists free and strode away, across the clearing and into the trees.

Bob grinned uneasily at the rest of us. 'Teenage daughters!' he said, as if it was all some kind of joke.

Wardle frowned. 'But if she and Matt have been conned—'

Scally kicked his ankle. 'Leave it, Wardie. It's not our problem, is it?'

Wardle shuffled his feet unhappily. 'Taco's a good little kid. We ought to go and sort out those crooks. Make them find some real stuff.'

'They're too far away,' Nobo said. He licked his lips nervously.

'So? We can hitch can't we? Got to do *something*.' Wardle stood up—but nobody else moved. And as he looked round, they all avoided his eyes.

I left them to it and went after Paige.

I'd guessed where she was going. It wasn't going to be fun telling Steff about her bike, but we had to do it. I struggled up the hill and slithered down the other side, trying not to think about anything except the brambles.

When I walked into Steff's house, she and Paige were sitting at the table, facing each other. Paige was talking very fast and Steff was leaning forward, watching her with eyes like steel. No yelling now. Just cold, silent fury.

Paige stopped and sat back and Steff said something short and very sharp—a question. Paige nodded and Steff jumped up and came towards me.

Ran towards me.

I flinched backwards, thinking she was going to hit me. But she didn't. She threw her arms round me and hugged me, talking very fast. When she stepped back, I could see tears in her eyes.

'She's sorry,' Paige said. 'Victor and his dad are French—so she's apologizing for them.'

'No!' I said. 'No, it's not her fault! Please tell her—'

Steff was watching my face, trying to understand what I was saying and I wanted her to know that *I* was sorry. Not just for losing her bike, but for everything I'd taken out of the barn. I wanted to make it up to her.

'Tell her I'll mend the rest of her bikes,' I said. 'I'll get the parts—somehow—and I'll do it for nothing. I won't leave her without a bike.'

When Steff heard that, she smiled and shook her head at me. Then she gave my shoulder a little push.

'Taco!' she said. And she flapped her hands at us both, to send us back to Lemon Dough.

22

As soon as we came out of the wood, we could see something happening in the bottom field. There were vans parked down there, and little groups of people moving about. Not drifting aimlessly, but striding around, as if they had work to do.

At first, we thought they'd brought us new tents. But when we were halfway down the hill I read some of the lettering on the vans.

'It's not tents,' I said. 'It's the TV people.'

Journalists with cameras were filming the heaps of ash—and the grubby children who were crowding round to watch them.

'Ghouls,' Paige said bitterly. 'We've lost the bikes, the camp's burnt, Taco's ill—and now they're taking pictures of it all. To amuse people who've still got homes and televisions.'

'It's not amusement,' I said. 'It's *news.*'

Paige pulled a face. 'So? They'll just take more pictures of pathetic, skinny children. That didn't change anything last time, did it?'

Last time—

'Hey!' I said. '*Hey!*' It came to me in a flash, and I started running for the gap in the fence.

'What is it?' Paige raced to catch up. 'What did you see?'

'Remember—' I turned round as I reached the fence. '—remember that journalist who talked to us? That man—what was he called?'

Paige understood straight away. 'Salman,' she said. 'He was called Salman something.' She followed me through the fence. 'But I can't see him.'

'He *must* be here!' I looked round frantically. 'You go up to the gate and I'll go across the field. Ask everyone!'

There were people everywhere. Two different TV crews were trying to film in the bottom field and everyone in the camp wanted to get into one picture or the other. I put my head down and charged into the crowd, yelling, 'Salman! Salman!' Just in case he could hear me.

I found him in the far corner of the field. His team had cleared a space for him, next to the blackened skeleton of one of the tents. He was talking into a camera, turning left and right to point to a couple of children with bandaged arms and legs.

I knew people would crowd towards him as soon as the filming was finished, so I didn't wait for that. I took a breath and launched myself forward straight away, flinging myself at all the people in between. The shock of it opened up a gap in front of me and I tumbled forward, on to the ground.

Right in front of Salman.

I heard the cameraman swear—not angry, but impatient—and I knew someone would be coming to move me, so I started shouting up at Salman before I'd even stood up.

'It's me! Please help me, Salman! There's nobody else. Please—'

He shook his head helplessly, hardly even glancing down. His eyes were sad, but I could see he was used to desperate people. *He's going to say no*, I thought. *He's just waiting for them to take me away.* I could feel someone coming up behind me and I reared up on my knees and yelled.

'Look at me properly, Salman! *Recognize* me!'

That surprised him. He looked down again—and this time his eyes changed. He *saw* me.

'Hey,' he said. 'You're that kid with the bike, aren't you? How's that cute little brother of yours?'

'He's dying,' I gabbled. 'Because there's no penicillin.

And—' I had to get it all out before the men grabbed me, but I couldn't tell him fast enough '—and I thought I'd got some—and they took my bike—but it was aspirin—they tricked me and—'

'He-ey,' Salman said again. And he held up his hand—but not to me. He was waving people back. And then he bent down and lifted me up, brushing the ash off my clothes. 'Tell me slowly,' he said. 'From the beginning.'

As I told him, he took out a little notebook and started jotting things down. When I got to the bit about Amy and the pills, he said, 'You're *sure* they're not penicillin?'

'She's a nurse,' I said. 'And she's sure.' Then I remembered. 'But we haven't told Taco they're fakes. Or my—my dad. Because if they *think* he's having penicillin, it might work anyway. And we haven't got anything else.'

Salman's fingers tightened on the pen and one of the crew leaned over and tapped the words he'd just written.

'There's your story, Sal,' he said.

Salman looked at me. 'There's got to be a story,' he said apologetically. 'If we run with it, we might be able to get some penicillin. Where is your brother?'

'He's in the sports centre,' I said. 'In a tiny little room.'

275

Salman nodded. 'Let's go and find him.'

He strode straight into the crowd and it parted for him as he and his crew headed up the hill. I jogged to keep up with them.

'*Please* don't tell Taco it's aspirin,' I said. 'Don't let him hear you talking about that.'

Salman looked round and grinned. 'He won't find out anything from my reporting—unless he speaks Arabic. Now, where's this *tiny little room?*'

I took him round the side of the building—with dozens of people trailing behind us—and opened the door a crack. Enough for Justin to see my face.

'How is he?' I said.

Justin rocked his hand. 'No better, no worse.'

Taco was lying curled up on the bed with his eyes half-open, gazing at the wall. I opened the door a little wider, so Salman could see over my shoulder, and I felt him stop breathing for a moment.

'I thought I was angry before,' he said softly. 'But now—'

Justin stood up. 'Who's this?' he muttered. 'What are you doing, Matt?'

'He can get help for Taco,' I said. 'Please—'

For a second I thought Justin was going to push everyone out and wreck it all. But Salman swung into action. He looked at Taco again and then beckoned to Justin.

'Please—can we speak outside?'

Justin hesitated for a second and then stepped through the door. 'I can't leave Taco for long. You can see how ill he is.'

'I'll watch him,' I said.

I went into the little room and shut the door, so Taco wouldn't hear anything. As I sat down, he stirred and opened his eyes.

'Matt,' he said. 'I'm hot.'

I picked the wet cloth out of the bucket by the bed and lifted him up so I could mop his face and the back of his neck. He felt so light it frightened me.

'Am I getting better?' he said.

I nodded firmly. 'You'll soon be well. And you've got a visitor. Remember the TV reporter who saw you riding my bike?'

'Good,' Taco said. 'He was a nice man.'

He lay back and closed his eyes and by the time Salman and Justin came back he was asleep again. Justin looked nervously at Salman.

'You'll be quick?' he said. 'I don't want him disturbed.'

Salman nodded. 'As soon as we've sorted the lights, we'll get a couple of shots and then I'll talk to you about what's wrong with him. We'll be gone before you know it.'

Taco didn't like the lights. His eyes flickered, without quite opening, and all the time Salman and Justin were talking he made small, unhappy noises. When the filming was finished, Salman leant over and put a hand on his forehead, smoothing his hair back.

'We're not supposed to get involved,' he said. 'But you can't stay human in this job unless you break the rules sometimes. I'll be back tomorrow.'

Justin nodded. He stood in the doorway, watching as Salman walked away down the hill. 'That's a man you can trust,' he said.

Salman did even more than he'd promised. The most I'd hoped for was some real penicillin, but three hours later, an ambulance drove into the camp. A couple of paramedics jumped out and came looking for Taco.

To take him to hospital.

When Justin muttered about the money, they brushed that aside. 'It's arranged,' one of them said. They lifted Taco gently on to a stretcher and signalled to Justin to follow them into the ambulance.

He looked at me and hesitated.

'Go *on*,' I said. 'I'll be fine here. I can stay with Muriel.'

I watched the ambulance drive away and then I went down the hill and curled up on the groundsheet in Muriel's tent. All I wanted was to fall asleep, but there were too many things churning around in my head. And around eleven, someone scratched on the flap at the back of the tent.

I stuck my head out and there was Paige, standing in the moonlight.

'Can I come in?' she whispered.

I lifted the flap to let her crawl through. 'You just disappeared,' I said. 'Where have you *been*?'

'Nowhere much. Up and down.' She was shivering and she sounded very tired. 'I kept thinking about Taco and wondering if he'll make it. Why do people keep *dying*?'

'He's not going to die,' I said. 'Salman sent an ambulance and he's gone to hospital. With Justin.'

'You should tell your mum,' Paige said. 'Just in case. Here.' And she held out her phone.

I looked at it. 'Are you sure? I can't give you anything.'

'It's a present,' Paige said. 'You can have as long as you like—till the credit runs out. Now stop wasting time and *phone* her.'

Mum answered straight away. 'Yes!' she said sharply. 'Who's that?'

'It's me, Mum,' I said. 'I—'

'What's going on?' she interrupted frantically. 'I keep texting Bob's phone, but there's never any answer.'

I saw Paige's eyes narrow.

'Bob hasn't given us any messages,' I said. 'But—'

Mum went plunging on. 'How is everyone? Is Justin's face better now? I've been so worried about him.'

'Yes, I think so,' I said. 'Justin's fine. But—'

'And Taco? Is he all right? He—'

I shouted down the phone. 'Be quiet and *listen*! No, Taco's not all right. He got bitten by a rat and—'

She was very quiet then, while I told her everything. I tried not to imagine how she must be looking. When I'd finished, there was a second of complete silence.

Then she said, 'It's his birthday on Friday.'

I didn't know that. It was hard to remember the date in Lemon Dough. And even if I had remembered—what could I have done for him?

'I think he's going to be all right,' I said. 'He's in hospital now and they'll give him penicillin.'

There was another silence. When Mum spoke again, her voice was so soft I could hardly hear it. 'I've sent him a present. And a letter. I want him to have a proper birthday. Will you make sure he gets them?'

'Yes,' I said. 'I'll make sure.'

'Promise?'

'I promise,' I said. 'I'll try and call you again very soon, to let you know how he is. OK?'

'And you too,' Mum said. 'How are you—really?'

'I'm—' *I'm fine* was what I wanted to say. But my mouth wouldn't make the words. 'I just wish I was home,' I muttered. 'I wish things were back the way they used to be.'

'Oh Matt,' Mum said. She took a long breath. 'Grandpa would have told you to remember what Einstein said.'

I didn't understand. 'You mean *e equals mc squared?*' I said.

She gave a fragile little laugh. 'No, not that one. The one Grandpa liked was, *Life is like a bicycle. If you want to stay balanced, you have to keep moving.* You remember that.'

'Yes,' I said. 'I'll remember it, Mum.'

'Good boy. Your dad would be proud of you.' She rang off very quickly, as if she couldn't manage to say any more.

I sat and looked at the phone until Paige reached over and took it out of my hand.

'No good staring at that,' she said. 'We have to *do* something.'

I blinked stupidly at her. 'Do something about what?'

'About Bob, of course.' She dropped the phone into her pocket and lifted the tent flap. 'We can't just let him get away with it. He has to be stopped. We'll make a plan in the morning.' She gave a brisk, determined nod and crawled out of the tent.

I lay down and pulled the blanket up over my shoulders. It felt very strange having the whole camp bed to myself. It took me a long time to fall asleep.

When I opened my eyes in the morning, the first thing I thought was, *How will I know what's happening to Taco?* There was no way of getting any news. Justin was stuck at the hospital, without a phone, and there was no way he could travel backwards and forwards. And if someone let him use a phone, the only number he knew was—Bob's.

If I'd had the bike, I would have cycled to the hospital. But I hadn't got it any more—because of Bob.

That was when I *really* started to feel angry. As if it had been smouldering away inside me all the time and suddenly it blazed up, in a great wall of flame. I'd trusted Bob and he'd tricked me and nearly killed Taco. Paige was right. We had to stop him swindling anyone else.

I scrambled up and crawled out of the tent. Muriel was stirring some kind of porridgey thing on the stove and jiggling Charlotte on her hip.

'Here,' she said. 'You can have some of this if you keep Charlotte quiet for five minutes. I daren't put her down. She's started crawling.'

'I need to go and find Paige,' I said.

'It won't hurt you to wait a bit,' Muriel said firmly. 'And you need some food. Don't suppose you ate anything yesterday. Here.'

She pushed Charlotte into my arms and started spooning out the stuff she was stirring into a couple of bowls. It looked disgusting, but everything Muriel cooked always tasted delicious. I sat down with Charlotte on my lap.

'She's getting heavier,' I said.

Muriel nodded. 'She'll soon be walking. That's going to be a whole new set of problems.' She sat down beside me and swapped Charlotte for one of the bowls. 'Now eat that. You'll need all your wits about you if you're going to tackle Bob.'

I stared at her. 'How—?'

'Think I'm deaf?' She gave me a sharp look. 'Are you sure he knew about those fake pills?'

'I'm sure,' I said.

'I don't think you'll convince other people. They all think he's the best thing since sliced bread. Be careful you don't get yourselves into worse trouble.'

I ate my porridge—it *was* delicious—and then went to look for Paige. It didn't take long, because she was on her way to find me. We met halfway up the field.

She looked dreadful. White-faced and shaky, as if she hadn't slept all night.

'What's the matter?' I said.

She rubbed a hand across her eyes. 'I know how we can stop Bob. There's only one way. We have to get him sent back to England.'

I didn't get it. 'How are we going to do that?'

'Oh, come *on*!' Paige said. 'Think! How did he get into Lemon Dough? Why didn't they put him straight on to the train back to England? Because—'

'Because you pretended to be his daughter.'

'Exactly!' Paige said. 'So now all I've got to do is go up to the sports centre and tell Bernadette—'

Now I understood why she looked so dreadful. 'You can't do that! They'll send you back too!'

'Serves me right, doesn't it?' Paige said bitterly. 'I should never have saved his skin. I knew who he was, the moment I first saw him.'

'Who he was? What—?' And then I remembered the name she'd called him in the woods. 'Super-Scadger,' I said slowly.

Paige laughed—a quick, angry little bark. 'He's got his own page on ScadgePost. You wouldn't believe the stuff they found in his house. There are lots of people looking for him.'

They're looking for us too, I wanted to say, but I couldn't find the words. And then Paige turned round, ready to start up the hill again, and I'd missed my chance.

I caught at her arm. 'Don't do anything yet. Let's think about it for a day or two. There must be another way, so *you* don't have to go back as well.'

'I've been thinking all night,' she said miserably.

But I could see she was hesitating, so I hunted for something to distract her. 'Look, why don't we go up to Steff's? I need to start fixing up one of those bikes. And someone ought to keep an eye on the vegetable patch now Justin isn't here. That's what we need—a bit of a break while we sort things out in our heads.'

'We-ell—'

She gave in, but I think it was only because she was too tired to argue. We trailed up the hill and into the woods and by the time Steff got home from taking Pierre to school we were both hard at work. I was mending a couple of punctures and Paige was on her hands and knees weeding round the gooseberries.

Steff took one look at her and let out a stream of French words. Then she caught hold of her shoulders and lifted her up. She led her into the house, nodding to me to follow, but I was just putting the patches on, so I finished that before I moved. By the time I went inside, Paige was fast asleep, with a piece of bread and jam in her hand.

Steff leaned over and stroked her hair. '*La pauvre*,' she said.

I didn't know what that meant, but I could guess. Paige looked very skinny and tired and grubby. What would she do if she went back to England? She had no money and no family—and Bob certainly wouldn't be looking after her.

I couldn't let it happen. There had to be another way.

23

STEFF GAVE ME a piece of bread and jam too, even though I did a Taco-style mime to show her I'd eaten. I took it out to the barn and went on working on the bike. I was determined to make it even better than the one Victor and his dad had bullied us into handing over.

It must have been two or three hours later when Paige and Steff came running into the barn. Paige was wide awake now and she pulled at my arm while Steff rattled on at me.

'Leave the bike,' Paige said. 'Steff wants to take us somewhere.'

My heart thudded. 'Is it Taco?'

Paige shook her head. 'No, it's something else— something special. If we don't hurry we'll miss it. Come *on*!'

Steff was signalling the same thing. So I pushed my tools into a corner and covered them over with some old polythene. Then I let Paige drag me into the pickup.

Steff didn't take the main road. She wove her way between the fields of sunflowers turning right, left, right on narrow tracks that were invisible until we reached them. Finally we came up against a barrier at a T junction and she parked at the side of the road and looked at her watch.

'*Vite!*' she said. '*Vite, vite, vite!*' She leaped out, beckoning to us to follow, and ran up to the junction.

There were half a dozen old men leaning on the barrier, chatting to each other. Steff asked them a question and they shook their heads and pointed up the road.

'What is it?' I said to Paige. 'What are we doing here?'

She grinned. 'It's a surprise. Come on.' And she pulled me up to the barrier.

We were just in time. A second later, a cluster of cars came down the road. One of them had a camera mounted on top, but I still didn't guess why Steff had brought me there. Not until all the cars were past.

Then, suddenly, half a dozen racing bikes came swooping towards us.

They were travelling at an unimaginable speed. Moving like birds in the air, like fish through the water. The pedals whirled round as if it took no effort at all to spin the wheels. The cyclists flashed by so fast I hardly had time to see them all. A heartbeat, and they were gone.

But it wasn't over. After a couple of seconds there were more bikes. And more. And more. A great gaggle of them, riding clumped up together, frighteningly close to each other—and to us. I could have reached out and touched the nearest one.

One of the old men did just that. He leaned forward and gave one of the cyclists a quick pat as he flew past. Then he turned and grinned at us, as if he had just seen the best sight in the world.

I watched the whole thing almost without breathing, desperate not to miss a single beautiful second. And when all the bikes had passed I leaned over the barrier and looked up the road, following them with my eyes.

They swung round a corner and disappeared, but I went on staring at the empty road, not wanting to lose them. Not wanting it to end.

That was where I wanted to be. Racing into the distance with all that beautiful French space unrolling in front of me. Maybe if I worked hard . . . if I saved enough money to buy a racing bike . . . if I trained and trained . . .

Steff leaned over and said something into my ear and when I looked round I saw her smiling at me.

'That was the *Tour de France*,' Paige said. 'She wants to know if you liked it.'

I drew a long breath before I could speak. 'Of course I liked it,' I said. 'Tell her it was the *best*. Tell her—'

But that didn't seem enough. I wanted to tell her myself, so she knew I really meant it. The right word felt strange in my mouth, but I made myself say it.

'*Merci*,' I said. '*Merci*, Steff.'

She laughed and patted my shoulder.

I didn't come back down to earth until Paige and I were walking back to the camp. Then as we came out on to the road, my dream of cycling into freedom crashed up against real life.

How could I disappear into the distance like that? I had no money, nowhere to go and no way of getting food. And I couldn't speak French.

The only place I could survive was Lemon Dough.

I'd always wondered why the soldiers didn't keep us shut in there, but now I understood. They knew we weren't all going to disappear into the French countryside—because we couldn't. We had to stay where people would feed us and give us shelter. Outside Lemon Dough, we'd be lost.

That was when the idea came to me. Very quietly, like the last piece of a puzzle sliding into place. I looked round at Paige.

'I know what we ought to do about Bob,' I said. 'He'll get what he deserves, but you won't have to go back to England.'

We stopped right there, on the edge of the road, and I told her what we were going to say to him.

We waited twenty-four hours, to make sure we had everything worked out perfectly. Then we went to find Bob.

He'd been lying low, spending most of the day outside the camp. And Paige had moved down into Muriel's tent, to avoid him. So we hadn't seen him at all for a couple of days. But we knew he'd wangled himself a place inside the sports centre. He wouldn't want to lose that, so he was sure to be there in the evening.

We went up when it was beginning to get dark. Paige waited in the car park and I slipped inside and found Bob in a corner, talking very quietly to a woman with two little boys. I don't know what he was saying, because he stopped as soon as he saw me.

'Paige is outside,' I said. 'She wants to talk to you.'

291

He gave me his familiar, easy smile, as if there was nothing wrong. 'Can't come just at the moment. I'm doing a bit of business.'

'You'll come,' I murmured. 'If you've got any sense.' I said it very lightly. Nothing heavy. But he got the message.

'My daughter's got some problem,' he said apologetically to the woman with the little boys. 'You know how it is. I'll be back in a minute.'

He sounded like a sensible, concerned father. If I hadn't known, I would never have guessed that he hadn't got any children.

Paige was over in the far corner of the car park, well away from the building—but close enough to the soldiers if things went wrong. Bob strode across to her, still playing the Perfect Parent.

'Is there something wrong?' he said.

Paige nodded, pressing her lips together. 'You know what's wrong,' she muttered. 'And *I* know what I'm going to do about it.'

Bob didn't react. But I could see him watching her, very closely. Waiting for what was coming.

'I can't go on pretending to be your daughter,' Paige said. 'Not after what you've done. I'm going in to see Bernadette, to tell her the truth.'

For a second Bob was very still. Then he said, 'Don't be silly. If they send me back, you'll have to go back too.'

Paige tossed her head. 'I don't care. I can't keep this up. It makes me sick.'

Bob looked round at me. 'Can't you talk some sense into her? She'll just be making a fool of herself. No one's going to believe her.'

'They will if we have a DNA test,' Paige said softly.

There was a small, cold silence.

My heart was pounding so fast I could hardly breathe. What would Bob do next? Would he try and negotiate? I was hoping he would. But suppose he didn't? Suppose he called our bluff?

He did something even worse. Suddenly he looked straight at me and said, 'I *can't* go back to England. Because I'm on ScadgePost—*just like you and Taco and Justin.*'

It sliced the air like a hatchet flying between me and Paige. I thought, *Why didn't I tell her when I had the chance? It's ruined everything.* I didn't dare look round at her, but I could feel her standing very still beside me and I braced myself. Waiting for her to yell at me and march off in disgust.

But she didn't. She took a long, slow breath. 'It's not the same thing,' she said, 'and you know it. You were scadging to make *money*. Matt and his family were just getting food to survive.' And she reached out sideways and caught hold of my hand, gripping it hard.

That was when Bob gave up on Lemon Dough. His eyes flickered for a second and then he said, 'Look—there's no need to make a drama out of all this. You're cutting off your nose to spite your face. Why don't I just go away from here? They won't miss me—as long as Paige keeps picking up the food vouchers. Isn't that better than getting us both sent back?'

Done it! I thought. Our plan had worked perfectly. We'd got Bob to suggest the answer we wanted—and made him think it was his own idea.

But Paige hadn't finished yet. She narrowed her eyes. 'You can't get off scot free like that. If you want me to keep quiet, you'll have to pay for those bikes.'

'No problem,' Bob said quickly. He took out his wallet.

Paige shook her head. 'Not that, I want French money.'

Bob slid the wallet back into his pocket. 'How much?'

'Tell you tomorrow morning,' Paige said. 'You'd better be at the gate at nine o'clock—ready to pay up—or I'll go straight to Bernadette. And tell her everything.'

'Suppose he sneaks away tonight?' I muttered.

Paige didn't take her eyes off Bob's face. 'He could risk it,' she said softly. 'But he might find the police coming after him. That would get in the way of your next lot of schemes—wouldn't it, Bob?'

Bob gave her a tight little smile. 'OK,' he said. 'We understand each other. I'll be there in the morning.'

Paige nodded briskly and headed off round the building. She was going so fast that I didn't catch up until she was almost at Muriel's tent. As I drew level with her, I could see her shaking with fury.

'I'm sorry,' I said. 'I'm sorry I didn't tell you—'

She stopped and shook her head. 'I'm not cross with *you*. I knew about that all the time. Recognized you all from ScadgePost, the first time I saw you.'

'So why didn't you say—?'

She gave me a twisted smile. 'How could I make a fuss? I'd just teamed up with Super-Scadger himself.'

'Well you've fixed him now,' I said. 'It's all over.'

'Not quite.' Paige started walking again. 'We have to go and see Scally now.'

'Why?'

'To ask how much the bikes were worth, of course. They know all about selling second-hand bikes.' She grinned. 'We don't want to swindle Bob, do we?'

We spent the evening in the woods, sitting round the fire with Scally and Nobo and Wardle. They were cooking sausages and Wardle gave us one of his to share.

'Got to look after your mates, haven't you?' he said.

'Business partners,' Scally said.

Nobo didn't say anything. But he listened very carefully while Paige explained about the bikes. Then he gave her a sharp look. 'Bob's agreed to pay up? How did you manage that?'

'Our secret,' Paige said. 'But don't worry. He'll pay. And then he's heading out of Lemon Dough for ever.'

'Well, he'd better not try coming here,' Wardle said gruffly. 'Not after what he did.'

'But what about the bikes?' said Scally. 'We've got a nice little business going, thanks to him.'

'Thanks to Matt,' Paige said. 'He's the one who does all the work. You'll be better off without Bob creaming off half the money.' She stood up. 'We'll come down and talk about it once he's right out of the way. Deal?'

'Deal,' said Scally, jumping up to shake her hand.

In the morning, Paige was more nervous than I expected. We went up to the gate early and Bob kept us waiting until the very last moment. By the time he appeared, she was biting her nails and looking round anxiously.

Bob didn't look worried at all. He had the money ready and he counted the notes out into her hand. Then he gave us both a nod and hoisted his bag on to his back.

'Be good,' he said cheerfully. 'Don't do anything I wouldn't do.'

He swung out through the gate and tramped away down the road with a spring in his step. As he went down the slope from Lemon Dough, he was whistling a bouncy little tune.

I thought Paige was going to pass out. 'He doesn't care at all!' she said furiously. 'We thought we were stopping his tricks, but he's just moving on to something new. And now I *can't* get him sent back to England, because I won't know where he is. He's fooled us!'

I wasn't so sure. He was at the bottom of the slope now and I stood and watched him climb up the next hill. Wasn't he just a bit *too* jaunty? As if he was trying to prove something? As he disappeared over the top of the hill, I grabbed Paige's arm. 'Come on,' I said. 'I want to see what he's like when he thinks he's out of sight.'

We ran out after him and walked quickly up to the top of the hill. When we came over the crest, he was much nearer than we expected. And there was nothing jaunty about him now. He was walking downhill quite slowly, dragging his feet a bit, as if the effort of putting on a show had exhausted him.

Paige looked down at him. 'If I didn't know what he'd done,' she said, 'I'd feel sorry for him now.'

I shook my head. 'He'll be OK. As soon as he's picked up a bit of French, he'll start scamming someone else, I expect. But we don't have to worry about him any more. Come on. Let's go and see Steff.'

But as we turned round, Steff came driving up the road towards us, on her way back from taking Pierre to school. When she saw us, she screeched to a stop and started talking very fast, pointing over her shoulder towards Lemon Dough.

Paige nodded and caught hold of my arm. 'She says they're putting up new tents in the bottom field. We ought to get back, to make sure you get one.'

'*Merci*,' I said. '*Merci*, Steff.' And we started hurrying down the hill.

It was Paige who spotted Justin. As we drew level with the camp, she gave a shout and pointed. 'Look! There's your dad!'

He was standing outside Muriel's tent, staring up towards the sports centre, as though he was searching for someone. Paige jumped up and down and waved to him.

'Yoo-hoo! Justin! Yoo-hoo!'

When he saw us, he started beckoning with both hands at once, as if he could scoop us towards him by pulling at the air. We ran the rest of the way—along the road and up through the gap in the fence—and he watched us, as though he could hardly bear to stand still.

'How's Taco?' I said, as soon as I was near enough to shout. 'Is he getting better?'

'Hurry up!' Justin shouted. 'You're missing his birthday!'

Paige started hanging back, but I caught her arm and made her come with me. We ran up to the tent together and Justin lifted the flap so that we could see inside.

Taco was sitting up in the nearest camp bed, with something in his hand and a parcel open on his lap.

'Happy birthday!' I said. 'What have you got there?'

'Mum sent them,' Taco said solemnly. 'I'm just deciding if I still like them.' And he bit into the taco he was holding.

Much later, when Taco was asleep, I went to sit outside the tent, to look up at the stars. I hadn't been there very long before Paige appeared.

'I've brought your money,' she said. 'What are you going to do about choosing a new bike? Want me to come and help you buy it?'

I stared up into the sky. 'I've been thinking about that,' I said. 'Maybe I won't buy a bike. Not just yet.

Then I could use the money to buy spares for repairing other people's bikes.' I looked sideways at her. 'But I'd need someone to share the business with me. Someone who speaks French.'

Paige leaned back on her elbows. 'Share a business with a scadger?' she said solemnly. 'That's a lot to ask. I'll only do it on one condition.'

'Which is?' I said warily.

'You've got to learn to speak French!'

I looked down the hill at the sunflower fields and the road that went on and on, into a whole, unknown country. *If you want to stay balanced, you have to keep moving.*

'OK,' I said. 'It's a deal.'